THEOLOGICAL DIALOGUE
BETWEEN ORTHODOX AND
REFORMED CHURCHES

THEOLOGICAL DIALOGUE BETWEEN ORTHODOX AND REFORMED CHURCHES

Edited by
THOMAS F. TORRANCE

1985

SCOTTISH ACADEMIC PRESS
EDINBURGH AND LONDON

Published by
Scottish Academic Press Ltd,
33 Montgomery Street
Edinburgh EH7 5JX

SBN 7073 0436 9

British Library Cataloguing in Publication Data
Torrance, Thomas F.
    Theological dialogue between orthodox and
    reformed churches.
    1. Theology, Doctrinal
    230   BT77.3

    ISBN 0-7073-0436-9

Printed in Great Britain by
Clark Constable, Edinburgh, London, Melbourne

CONTENTS

PREFACE

The different papers that comprise this volume were read at three Consultations between Orthodox and Reformed Churchmen and Theologians, at Istanbul, July 26-30, 1979, at Geneva, February 15-18, 1981, and again at Geneva, March 6-11, 1983. The account of these Consultations offered in the Introduction relies not only on my own notes of these sessions but also, and very heavily, upon the meticulous records kept by the Reverend Richmond Smith, then Secretary of the Department of Theology of the World Alliance of Reformed Churches, and upon the correspondence dating back to 1976 relating to these Consultations. I have not had access to the corresponding records at the Ecumenical Patriarchate at Fener, Istanbul, but the minutes and historical records provided by the Rev. Richmond Smith have been available to the secretariat at Fener which has not drawn our attention to any discrepancy between the records at Geneva and at Istanbul. The account of the Consultations inevitably reflects my own personal point of view. Since it was impossible to give even a summary of all the contributions made over these years, I have studied the records of each of them and offered a digest of the significant points that emerged in the light of the whole series. While many interesting themes are thus inevitably omitted, it is hoped that the consistent thrust of the intention and argument running through the Consultations has been thrown into relief in a form that does justice to them. I am further deeply in the debt of Richmond Smith for checking over what I have written.

I should like to take this opportunity to express my personal gratitude to His All-Holiness Dimitrios I, the Archbishop of Constantinople and Ecumenical Patriarch, and to his Bishops and Theologians in Istanbul and Geneva, from whom I have had the greatest help and kindness. I am no less indebted to Their Beatitudes the Patriarchs of Alexandria and Jerusalem, and the Archbishops of Athens and Cyprus who, together with their Bishops and Theologians, gave me such an encouraging welcome, and bestowed their blessing upon the Reformed initiative to open up Dialogue.

Finally, sincere thanks are due to His Eminence Archbishop Methodios of Thyateira and Great Britain for allowing me to republish the 'Memoranda on Orthodox/Reformed Relations' presented at Istanbul, which he had earlier published in *Ekklesia kai Theologia*, Vol. I (1980), pp. 197-211; and likewise to Dr. Sergei Hackel, who had published the notable paper by Chrysostomos Konstandinidis, Metropolitan of Myra, 'Authority in the Orthodox Church', in *Sobornost*, Vol. 3, no. 2 (1981), pp. 197-209. The Rev. Archimandrite John H. Maitland Moir of Edinburgh, and the Rev. Richmond Smith, now of Kipford, Kirkcudbrightshire, have given me careful help with the proofs, for which I am most grateful.

The publication of this book is sponsored and supported jointly by The Ecumenical Patriarchate in Istanbul and The World Alliance of Reformed Churches centred in Geneva. Its actual production has been made possible by generous subventions from Mr. Reo Stakis of Glasgow and Mr. Harry G. Kuch of Philadelphia, for which the sponsors and contributors express their warm appreciation. The editor would like to express his gratitude also for the encouragement extended to him by Dr. James I. McCord, Chairman and Chancellor of the Center of Theological Inquiry in Princeton, and by Mr. Douglas Grant of The Scottish Academic Press in Edinburgh.

Edinburgh,   Thomas F. Torrance
Advent 1983.

INTRODUCTION

T. F. TORRANCE

Theological conversations between Orthodox and Reformed Churches have been taking place in various parts of the world for some time. They go back to contacts formed during the early period of the Ecumenical Movement, especially since the epoch-making Missionary Conference held in Edinburgh in 1910 and the first two Conferences on Faith and Order held in Lausanne in 1927 and in Edinburgh in 1937 which contributed so effectively toward the formation of the World Council of Churches. However, it was with the First Assembly of the World Council of Churches at Amsterdam in 1948 and the Third World Conference of Faith and Order at Lund in 1952 that serious theological dialogue between Orthodox and Reformed Churchmen began to take place, not least through the ten years' work of the Special Commission on Christ and his Church appointed at Lund, in which both Professor Chrysostomos Konstantinides (now the Metropolitan of Myra) and I took part. Particular mention must be made of the impact on this dialogue of the late Very Rev. Professor Georges Florovsky, whose profound theological instinct, at once catholic and evangelical, and whose Christocentric and Trinitarian interpretation of Greek Patristic Theology won the admiration and inspired the lasting confidence of his Reformed colleagues.

After the Fourth World Conference of Faith and Order held at Montreal in 1962 formal conversations between the World Alliance of Reformed Churches and Orthodox Churches began to take place: in Rumania through representatives of the Orthodox and Reformed Churches since 1964; in North America through theologians from the Standing Conference of Canonical Orthodox Bishops in the Americas and Reformed Churches in Canada and the United States since 1968; and in Eastern Europe under the aegis of the Moscow Patriarchate and the World Alliance of Reformed Churches, in Hungary since 1972 and in the Soviet Union since 1976. In the same year steps were also taken through the Secretariat of the World Alliance of Reformed Churches in Geneva, and its Department of Theology, to open up theological consultations with the Greek Orthodox Church, but with a rather different objective from that of the other Church conversations just mentioned.

The impetus for this new move came from a deep theological rapport that had developed between Archbishop Methodios of Aksum (as he then was) and myself over the understanding of classical Alexandrian theology, as represented above all by St. Athanasius and St. Cyril, and our appreciation of its scientific basis. In 1969 Archbishop Methodios had refounded the ancient Journal of Historical Greek Theology, *Ekklesiastikos Pharos*, and in 1970 had founded a new Journal, *Abba Salama*, with a view to clarifying the foundations of the Greek Conciliar Theology upon which all Christendom had come to rest, and with a view also towards reconciling Chalcedonian and non-Chalcedonion theology, in all of which I had come to be deeply associated. In 1970 formal contact was established between the Patriarchate of Alexandria and the Church of Scotland, when Nicholaos VI, Pope and Patriarch of Alexandria, accompanied by the Archbishops of Aksum and of Thyateira and Great Britain visited the General Assembly of the Church of Scotland; and three years later I was invited to join Archbishop Methodios in lectures and addresses given in Addis Ababa, in thankful commemoration of Athanasius the Great who died in A.D. 373. Since, apart from personal friendships that had grown up over the years, these contacts had been brought about and continued to be sustained by profound theological accord, it seemed right that an attempt should be made to engage in formal theological consultations with the Ecumenical Patriarchate with a view to clarifying together the classical bases of Orthodox and of Reformed theology and in the hope of reaching the same kind of profound accord with respect to the 'theological axis' of Athanasian/Cyriline theology, to which the Reformed Church has looked as having regulative force in its understanding of Christian doctrine hardly less than the Greek Orthodox Church.

In submitting a proposal along these lines to the World Alliance of Reformed Churches, I suggested that I might personally carry the proposal to his All-Holiness, Dimitrios I,

the Archbishop of Constantinople and Ecumenical Patriarch,
and discuss it also with the Heads of the Greek Orthodox
Church in the Middle East, during a visit I hoped to make as
Moderator of the General Assembly of the Church of Scotland.
In agreeing to the proposal, the Executive Committee of the
World Alliance of Reformed Churches under its President, Dr.
James I. McCord of Princeton, gave me the freedom to present
the proposal personally to the Patriarch and the other Heads of
the Greek Church along the lines I thought appropriate. I had
in mind fundamental theological dialogue beginning with the
doctrine of the Holy Trinity in which discussion would centre
upon the teaching of Athanasius and Cyril rather than upon the
Cappadocians, who seemed to have occupied the main
attention of Orthodox theologians in recent years, for in that
way I believed we could cut behind certain disagreements
between Eastern and Western theology, not least relating to the
filioque clause of the Western Creed. Then from that basis I
considered we could move on to fuller accord regarding the
doctrines of Christ, the Holy Spirit, the Church, the Sacraments
and the Ministry than we could otherwise.

In due course a formal letter from the Alliance signed by
Professor Jan M. Lochman, Chairman of the Department of
Theology, to his All-Holiness, Dimitrios I, was entrusted to me
to convey to him. This letter expressed the desire of the Alliance
of Reformed Churches to explore the possibility of structured
theological conversations, and authorised me to speak to these
concerns in person.

Here is the letter in full.

His Holiness Dimitrios I
Archbishop of Constantinople and
Ecumenical Patriarch   Feb. 18, 1977

Your Holiness,
I write this letter of personal greeting with pleasure and
with a sense of thanksgiving. That the bearer, the present
Moderator of the General Assembly of the Church of
Scotland, the Right Rev. Prof. T. F. Torrance is able to
visit Your Holiness in his capacity as representative of the
Church of Scotland is a source of satisfaction to many of
us of the Reformed family of Churches. We greatly value

these and similar contacts, not only for what they represent in themselves but as sign-posts towards that fuller fellowship to which we believe God is calling His people everywhere.

The occasion of such a visit has prompted a number of us who have the theological interest of the Church at heart to avail ourselves of this opportunity of conveying to you the greetings of many in the Reformed family of Churches who are concerned to seek that day when the visible unity of the One Church Catholic will become a witness to all men of the Gospel of Jesus Christ.

As you are possibly aware, the Reformed family of Churches numbers today 143 autonomous denominations throughout the world with approximately 60 million communicant church members. The distinctive characteristics of the Reformed churches can be traced through the theological and historical development, linked with names such as Jan Hus of Bohemia, Ulrich Zwingli and John Calvin of Switzerland and John Knox of Scotland, and many others associated with them. Principally it was the work of John Calvin in the 16th century which has shaped much of the life of the majority of Reformed Churches as we know them today. As you also most assuredly know, the theology of Calvin was deeply rooted in patristic thought and doctrine, embracing the early Fathers both of the East and the West. The great ecumenical councils and creeds of the Ancient Church are received in our own tradition as they are in yours. And yet, in the historic development of Christendom the Reformed family of Churches and the Orthodox Churches have not infrequently found contact and fellowship one with the other to be difficult.

In recent years, however, we have seen with much appreciation a movement of rapprochement in understanding. In North America the first phase of Reformed/Orthodox dialogue published in 1973 a volume of reports entitled *The New Man*, edited by John Meyendorff and Joseph McLelland.

In Eastern Europe conversations between Orthodox and Reformed have progressed in Rumania. In 1972 in

Debrecen, Hungary, there was a discussion between representatives of the Moscow Patriarchate and representatives of Reformed Churches and this was followed by a larger meeting in Leningrad, October 20-24, 1976, a communiqué of which meeting is enclosed for your interest.

Concerning relations between Reformed Churches and the Roman Catholic Church, you will be interested to know that the Reformed family is now in process of concluding a series of theological dialogues on two distinct subjects (The Theology of Marriage and The Presence of Christ in Church and World) which in the last six years have been officially sponsored between the World Alliance of Reformed Churches and the Secretariat for Promoting Christian Unity of the Roman Catholic Church, the Vatican. We expect these final reports to be available in 1977. In this context I wish to add that from time to time our theological investigations with our brethren of the Roman Catholic Church have reminded us together of our common heritage in the ancient undivided Church to which your own tradition also looks for its source and origin. Many of us are convinced that a fresh rediscovery of the biblical and patristic foundation of the faith is one of the essential needs of many churches of today as they endeavour to live out the obedience of the Gospel.

Bearing all these considerations in mind it is our hope and prayer that in the years to come theologians of Reformed Churches and of your own Church may increasingly enter into fruitful exchange. Such contacts can indeed be developed in many different ways and on different levels in the life of the Church, theological study, exchange of visiting professors, etc. Much of this development is no doubt best furthered by allowing it to proceed according to the commitment and initiative of individual theologians.

However, in order to represent more effectively the wholeness of our respective traditions and Christian witness, would it not be appropriate for us to consider various means of some kind of structured conversations between representatives from your Church and from the

Reformed family of Churches? At this stage I only raise the question; but I do so in the knowledge that repeatedly the World Alliance of Reformed Churches through General Councils and Executive Committees has affirmed its commitment to a closer understanding with all Orthodox Churches.

On this specific issue of how best to develop Reformed/Orthodox dialogue I shall look forward with great interest to your reply once you have had due time to consider the various possibilities which may be open. Indeed should you wish to discuss this matter with the present bearer of this letter, Dr. Thomas F. Torrance, I shall be happy to hear from him your own immediate first reaction. However, I quite appreciate that only later after careful consideration on both sides can we proceed to consider together a specific proposal for future contacts.

I conclude this letter with the prayer that the Holy Spirit may ever continue to guide and lead us, as indeed our Lord and Master promised to the first disciples that the Spirit would come upon the Church.

Animated with this hope I assure Your Holiness of our cordial greetings, in the name of Jesus Christ, our Lord, whom we seek to serve,

I am,
Yours very sincerely,
Jan M. Lochman
Chairman of the Department of Theology

Accompanied by my wife I visited his All-Holiness Dimitrios at Fener, Istanbul, during the second week of March, 1977, when we were cordially and royally received by the Patriarch himself, and also by his Bishops including my old friend Professor Konstantinidis, now Bishop of Myra and President of the Orthodox Commission for Inter-Christian Affairs. They reacted very warmly to the letter from the World Alliance of Reformed Churches, and to my explanation of the way we proposed that Dialogue between us should begin with the doctrine of the Holy Trinity, in the hope that we might be able together to do something ecumenically significant, not just for relations between the Reformed and Orthodox Churches, but for the whole Church Catholic and Evangelical in East and West.

From Istanbul we went to Athens where I was graciously received by Archbishop Seraphim, and then, accompanied by Archbishop Methodios, we went to Cyprus as the guest of Archbishop Makarios, and on to Cairo and Alexandria, to a very gracious reception by His Beatitude Nicholaos VI, Pope and Patriarch of Alexandria and All Africa, when for several days I enjoyed good theological discussion with his Bishops and theologians about the Alexandrian contribution to the foundations of classical Christian theology. Finally, we flew on to Jerusalem, 'the Mother of the Faithful', and were very warmly received by His Beatitude Benedictos, the venerable Greek Orthodox Patriarch of Jerusalem, who, with Archbishop Vasilios and Archbishop Germanos, gave me a deeply sympathetic and encouraging hearing. Thus all the Heads of the Greek Orthodox Church whom I visited in the Middle East, to whom I had the privilege of conveying greetings from the Ecumenical Patriarch, responded no less approvingly than His All-Holiness Dimitrios to our Reformed initiative.

In due course I reported back to the Officers of the World Alliance of Reformed Churches in Geneva, while the Ecumenical Patriarch through his personal representative at the World Council of Churches, Metropolitan Emilianos of Selybria extended to the President of the Alliance, President James I. McCord of Princeton Theological Seminary, an invitation to lead a Reformed delegation of theologians to visit the Ecumenical Partiarchate in Istanbul. This invitation was unanimously accepted by the Executive Committee of the Alliance at its session in Geneva in August 1978, when President James I. McCord appointed the following persons to join him in this delegation: Prof. Jan M. Lochman, Chairman of the Department of Theology, Professor T. F. Torrance from Scotland, Professor Hans-Helmut Esser from the Federal Republic of Germany, Professor Joe McLelland from Canada, Prof. Istvan Juhasz from Rumania, Dr. Edmond Perret, General Secretary of the Alliance, and the Rev. Richmond Smith, its Theological Secretary. Unfortunately, owing to circumstances beyond his own control, Professor Juhasz was unable to take part in this visit or to participate in any of the consultations that followed. A corresponding delegation was appointed by the Ecumenical Patriarchate consisting of the following: Metropolitan Chrysostomos Konstantinidis of Myra, as Leader, Metropolitan Konstantinos of Derka, Professor Vasil Anagnostopoulos, Professor Vasil Istavridis, the Rev. Deacon Chrysostomos Kalavdjis, the Rev. Deacon Apostolos Danilidis, and Mr. George Lemopoulos. Not all these representatives were able to participate in subsequent conversations, but the Metropolitan of Myra remained the Head of the Orthodox delegation and the Co-Chairman along with President McCord.

In due course this first consultation between Orthodox and Reformed Theologians and Churchmen took place at Fener, Istanbul, over a five-day period, from July 26 to July 30, 1979. It was a very memorable and joyful event in which all who took part were conscious of the historic significance of what was happening. This was clearly reflected in the formal addresses of the respective chairmen on July 26.

The address delivered by President James I. McCord of the World Alliance of Reformed Churches:

Your All-Holiness,
First of all, we Reformed are grateful for the Ecumenical leadership of the Orthodox Church. It is now more than 50 years since the call came from this historic Throne to Christians to unite. And one of the great blessings that has come to me in 30 years with the Ecumenical Movement has been working with Orthodox colleagues. One of those is my neighbour and colleague, who is under Your jurisdiction, Professor Georges Florovsky.
The second thing I want to say is that the Reformed have historically felt very close to the Orthodox, because of your concern and our concern for the Apostolic Faith. We think of you as the Church of the Holy Spirit, and John Calvin, one of our ancestors, has been called the theologian of the Holy Spirit.
And the third thing is the family that we represent; the Reformed and the Presbyterian is the most international

of all Protestant families. We go by different names in
different parts of the world. On the continent of Europe,
we are called Reformed, because in the 16th century
Reformation the dominant issue was the Faith. Our
Church was then called first in France the Church of
Jesus-Christ reformed according to the Word of God. In
the British Isles, the problem tended to be one of polity or
government, and, therefore, the name Presbyterian was
given to us. We now represent nearly 150 autocephalous
Churches around the world. Because of the commitment
of the Reformed family to the whole *Oikumene*, we look
forward to these days with You and Your Commission in
Istanbul and to the opportunity to discuss with You the
historic Apostolic Faith.

We pray for the blessing of the Holy Spirit on our
discussion. We pray for the continued blessing of the Holy
Spirit on You and Your people. You are very much in the
thoughts and prayers of the Reformed world.

And we are grateful to God for Your heroic leadership
of the faithful from this historic Patriarchate.

Address by His All-Holiness Dimitrios I, The Ecumenical
Patriarch:

Reverend and Honourable Sirs,
The President, The General Secretary and representatives
of the World Alliance of Reformed Churches.

Welcome to this city and to this historic Throne, which
is the First of Eastern Orthodoxy. It is the first in the
general structure of the Orthodox Church. It is especially
so in the diaconia of the other Churches, and in its
contribution to strengthening 'the unity of the Spirit in
the bond of peace' (Eph.) among the Churches and
among all men of good will.

We greet you in love and we receive you with great
honour. You represent in the most official way the large
and well-respected world of the Reformed Churches. You
came here with the sacred and concrete purpose of
making the official proposal for the opening of the
Theological Dialogue with Orthodoxy. We shall
favourably study this proposal and we shall forward it

properly to all other Orthodox Churches in the spirit of service to the great cause of unity.

You have the great responsibility of representing the highest Body of the Reformed Churches, which is the World Alliance. You hold different posts, the most significant in the administration and in the theological thought of this Body. At this moment the two great Families, of the Presbyterians and of the Congregationalists, and more than 140 Reformed Churches and Confessions, from Europe, from North and Latin America, from Asia, from Africa and Australasia, have turned their attention to this important visit of their Representatives.

To the great dates of your uniting movement of the last hundred years, i.e., the years 1875, 1891 and 1970, we think that you are adding with your visit and with your proposal the present year 1979 also. This will remain reciprocally as a historical point in the relations of our Churches.

The millions of your faithful are waiting for a positive response to their wholehearted wish and desire for the meeting, cooperation and growing-together in Dialogue with Orthodoxy.

Even if there were no common points of agreement between you and us on matters of faith, practice and tradition — which is certainly not the case — the two sides will have the opportunity through their contact and dialogue to discover and underline such common points which will prove valuable to both of us.

The desire and the turning to the East since the time of Calvin and Zwingli up to the present is historically witnessed.

On our side the wish and prayer for rapprochement and the 'unity of all' has always been constant.

We must proceed to the Dialogue with good will, with courage, with hope. 'Hope maketh not ashamed' (Rom. 5, 5). And the Lord never belies those expectations put upon Him.

Addressing you again with a warm welcome, we assure you that we shall look forward with interest and trust to the fruits of the conversations which you will have in these days with our Synodical Commission on Inter-Christian Affairs.

Let the Lord be your help and inspirer in your common efforts. So be it!

In his remarks opening the dialogue Metropolitan Chrysostomos pointed out that it was in his capacity as President of the standing Commission for Inter-Christian Relations that he had been appointed to lead the Orthodox Delegation. That indicated the significance he attached to the dialogue. He spoke frankly of the fact that the Orthodox had always regarded the Reformed as a protest against the Western Establishment and as part of the schism of the Western Church. At the same time the Orthodox recognised the Reformed concern for the truth and witness of the Early Church. It was rather a paradox that while the Reformed were part of the schism of the West, they had nevertheless borne consistent witness to their concern for the unity of the one Church, grounded in the Apostolic Faith. The Metropolitan expressed the appreciation of the Orthodox for the work of the Reformed Churches in the Alliance in bilateral and multilateral conversations that had been features of recent years. He went on to say how happy the Orthodox were in their belief that the time was right for dialogue between the Orthodox and the Reformed. This was surely due to the prompting of the Holy Spirit. It was on that basis that the dialogue should go forward, and with the prayer that God would bless their work together.

In response Dr. McCord expressed the gratitude of his Reformed Colleagues for the assurance of the Orthodox as to their commitment to think, pray and speak together of the Faith once delivered to the Apostles and of the nature of the Church, all to the glory of God. After explaining the nature of the commission and authority of the Reformed Delegation, he stressed the fact that he and his Colleagues were eager for the dialogue in the conviction that the Orthodox Church had much to give to the *Oikumene* as a whole, and directed his Orthodox partners to the Reformed convictions and proposals expressed in the memoranda prepared for them by Professor Torrance, to be considered in due course. Meantime he wished to confirm their common belief that the Spirit of God was mightily at work in what they were seeking to do together. We are not called, he added, to design the end, but to be faithful to the promptings of the Spirit. The world appeared to be drifting towards re-tribalisation, but the Church was seen to be drawing more closely together. It was a fruitful sign that East and West were found talking together, but in all that they did they must let themselves be talked to by the Scriptures, by the Creeds, and by the Holy Spirit in their midst.

Before the Conference embarked upon its main task — the discussion of two theological memoranda put forward by the Reformed Delegation — Professor Istavridis, as a Church Historian, presented an account of how the Orthodox had been accustomed to think of the Calvinist Reformation, and offered a brief résumé of relations between the Orthodox and the Reformed from the time of the Patriarch of Constantinople Cyril Loukaris (1572-1638) to the present day. This gave rise to a particularly helpful session in which Orthodox and Reformed participants were to see each other from the others' point of view and to clear away any incidental misunderstandings. At the same time, Professor Istavridis described the favourable reaction of the Holy Synod to the report submitted to it on June 24, 1977, by the Committee on Inter-Christian Relations concerning the approach of the World Alliance of Reformed Churches to the Ecumenical Patriarchate, and the formal proposal for theological conversations personally conveyed to his All-Holiness Dimitrios I through Professor Torrance, including the preference that discussions might begin with the dogma of the Holy Trinity. The following recommendation of the Committee had been adopted by the Synod:

'Our Committee, having studied all the data available, related to the contacts and the proposed theological Dialogue between Orthodox and Reformed Churches, does not ignore the significance of this matter. Neither does it differentiate this Dialogue from the rest which have already been started and are being continued, or from those that it has been planning for and keeps up and especially at inter-Orthodox level; yet it has some reservations. Therefore it would respectfully state that its

members are convinced that it would be better if the
Mother Church would simply allow that a phase of
informal theological contacts and meetings between
Orthodox and Reformed Churches opened, as has
hitherto been the case with relations between Orthodox
and Lutherans. The beginning of a formal theological
dialogue should follow later in due time, meanwhile
putting into practice the already known mechanism of
inter-Orthodox activation of things.'

In the discussions that followed several points of significance
were clarified and established. While there was full agreement
on the part of the Orthodox that theological conversations
should go ahead, it was felt that in the first instance these should
have an exploratory character, in the hope that, if sufficiently
close agreement appeared possible, formal theological dialogue
would follow between representatives of the Churches of the
Reformed Alliance and all fourteen Orthodox Churches. These
exploratory conversations would take place under the aegis and
with the full support of the Ecumenical Patriarchate and the
Holy Synod which in due course, it was hoped, would make firm
proposals to all the Orthodox Churches of the Pan-Orthodox
Synod. At the same time the Reformed Delegation would seek
the authorisation of the World Alliance of Reformed Churches
through its Executive Committee to proceed along the lines of
mutual agreement reached among the representatives of the
Orthodox and Reformed Churches at Istanbul. It was fully
accepted by all that discussions should begin with the doctrine of
the Holy Trinity so that if full and firm consensus could be
reached there, a regulative base would be provided for
continuing conversations. They would be officially known as
Theological Dialogue between Orthodox and Reformed Churches.

At that first meeting in Istanbul considerable attention was
given to problems of method and the underlying assumptions
that gave rise to divergence in doctrinal formulation and in the
structure of the ministry in the historical developments of
Catholic and Evangelical Churches. It was generally agreed
that method and theme should be kept in the closest possible
relation, so that the truth-content of the Gospel would be
allowed to control its expression and the Trinitarian substance

of the Faith would be given its regulative force in all theological formulation. In this event, however, attention must be given to the clarification of Orthodox and Reformed understanding of authority and its function in reaching doctrinal consensus in the Church on the ground of its Apostolic Foundation in Christ. This would inevitably mean, as Metropolitan Chrysostomos indicated, that the question of 'Apostolic practice' would have to be raised, for basic differences in the understanding of the ministry could not be avoided. Thus in due course theological dialogue centred in the doctrine of the Holy Trinity would have to have on its agenda matters of Order as well as of Faith. Since the Orthodox felt that they needed to have from the Reformed further clarification of their understanding of authority if discussions were to be fruitful, and since the Reformed, for whom all essential matters of Order are held to be *de fide*, felt that it would be helpful if the Orthodox gave them a theological account of authority, it was readily agreed that the next stage in these preparatory theological discussions would be devoted to this theme.

After these proposals had been officially mandated both by the Ecumenical Patriarchate and by the Executive Committee of the World Alliance of Reformed Churches, the second consultation between Orthodox and Reformed theologians took place at the John Knox International Reformed Centre in Geneva from February 15 to February 18, 1981. This time Metropolitan Chrysostomos of Myra was accompanied by Metropolitan Emilianos of Selybria, the permanent Representative of the Ecumenical Patriarch at the World Council of Churches, and by Metropolitan Damaskinos of Tranoupolis, the Head of the Orthodox Centre of the Ecumenical Patriarchate at Chambésy-Geneva, as well as by Mr. George Lemopoulos. The Reformed representatives led by President James I. McCord, remained the same, but again with the absence of Professor Istvan Juhasz of Rumania. Since the discussions were still to be of an interim, preparatory, nature, it was decided that no attempt to draft even tentative agreements at this point would be needed.

Three papers were presented: by Metropolitan Emilianos entitled *God's Immutability and Communicability*, in response to Professor Torrance's two Memoranda at Istanbul; by Professor

Hans-Helmut Esser on *The Authority of the Church and Authority in the Church, according to the Reformed Tradition*; and by Metropolitan Chrysostomos on *Authority in the Orthodox Church*.

In the wide-ranging discussions that followed each of these papers Orthodox and Reformed participants· alike kept returning to the need for a dynamic understanding of the living, Triune God in the inseparability of his Being and Act. Through the incarnation of the Son and in the outpouring of the Holy Spirit, each of whom is *homoousios*, or of one and the same Being, with him, God the Father is revealed as personally and actively participant in the Church and in the life of each member. Through the Son and in the Spirit we are given access to God himself, while in the Spirit and through the Son, it is not something of himself that God in his grace gives to us and makes known to us, but his very Self as God the Father Almighty, Creator of heaven and earth and of all things visible and invisible. Since what God reveals to us in this way he is inherently in his own eternal Being, and what he is in his own eternal Being he is toward us in Jesus Christ and his Spirit, the ultimate criterion of truth with which we operate in the Church cannot be anything other than, or less than, God himself. The *kanōn tēs alētheias* is the *Alētheia* himself, the Word of God made flesh in Jesus Christ, embodied in the midst of his Church, but this has to be understood not only in its 'vertical' dimension in the relation between God and mankind, but also in its 'horizontal' dimension as the presence and power and authority of the incarnate Truth of God within space and time, that is, within the on-going life and activity of the Church, which is the Body of Christ, indwelt by his Spirit.

During the discussion considerable consensus emerged between the Reformed position expounded by Professor Esser and the deeply Christocentric approach to authority functioning through 'communion' at all levels in the Church advocated by Metropolitan Chrysostomos. Stress was also laid upon the role of the Holy Spirit as the divinely-appointed authority to guide the Church into all truth; but the combination of this with the pattern of authority set by Our Lord as one of 'communion', called for a rethinking of all ecclesial, episcopal and synodical authority, which would take seriously the function of consensus in the Church as it was exteriorised in the 'catholic, universal reality of the Councils'. If some measure of genuine agreement was to be reached, however, it was generally agreed that we must start not from the doctrine of the Church and the authority of its ministry but from a centre deep in the doctrine of the Holy Trinity, and from that central position work out its implications for doctrines of the Church, Ministry, Authority, Sacraments and so on. Such a programme of work would be of very considerable help in a wider ecumenical scene beyond the concerns of the interrelations between the Orthodox and Reformed Churches alone. It was then resolved that in the succeeding consultation, to take place in two years time, the theme would be: *The Trinitarian Foundation and Character of the Faith and of Authority in the Church*. It was also agreed that particular attention should be given to the Niceno-Constantinopolitan Creed as exhibiting the Church's understanding not only of the Holy Trinity but of the way in which the canon of truth and authority actually operated in the decisions of the Church. It was hoped that both Orthodox and Reformed Delegations would then be in a position to propose to their respective authorities that fully structured dialogue might begin.

In due course the third consultation took place again in Geneva, but this time in the Orthodox Centre of the Ecumenical Patriarchate at Chambésy, from March 6 to 11, 1983. Metropolitan Chrysostomos of Myra, as hitherto, led the Orthodox Delegation, consisting of the Metropolitans Emilianos of Selybria, Damaskinos of Tranoupolis, Vasilios of Aristi from Germany, Father John Breck and Father Gennadios Limouris, both from France, and Mr. George Lemopoulos. Owing to the serious illness of his wife Dr. James I. McCord had resigned from the Reformed Delegation, but his place as Leader was taken by Professor Jan M. Lochman, while Professors Hans-Helmut Esser, Joe McLelland and Thomas F. Torrance were now joined by Dr. Lukas Vischer, the new Chairman of the Department of Theology in the World Alliance of Reformed Churches, and Dr. Edmond Perret, the General Secretary of the Alliance, together with the Rev. Richmond Smith, its Theological Secretary. The conference had before it two papers which had been distributed in advance, one by Professor T. F. Torrance, entitled *The Trinitarian Foundation and Character of*

Faith and of Authority in the Church, and one by Metropolitan Emilianos, entitled *The Trinitarian Structure of the Church and its Authority*.

A very full and frank theological discussion took place, throughout which the Trinitarian substance of the Faith was allowed to shape and control thought about the nature and operation of Authority. While a subordinationist element in the doctrine of the Trinity, together with a conception of hierarchical order within God, would appear to lie behind authoritarian and Caesaropapalist notions of the Church, a doctrine of the Holy Trinity as a consubstantial Communion of Love between Father, Son and Holy Spirit, without any subordinationism, implied a very different conception of authority and its mediation through Christ in the foundation of the Church and through the *koinonia* of the Spirit. Moreover such a view of authority embodied in Christ and the Church united to him must take a corporate form. In the discussion this was associated with the concept of the Truth of God as embodied in Christ and as taking an embodied form in the Apostolic Foundation of the Church and the Deposit of Faith handed down through Apostles. But because Truth and Authority have to do with God himself, the Supreme Truth and the Supreme Authority, it is the *Autoalētheia* and the *Autoexousia* of God's own Triune Being that must be recognised as the ultimate Judge in all our knowledge of him and in all our ministry and service in the Church. It was clear, however, that there were divergences on the nature of embodied authority in the Church and the way it functions, though there was general agreement that this had to be thought out in terms of communion, grounded in the union between the Church and Christ and ultimately in the Consubstantial Communion of the Holy Trinity.

Other problems were thrown up in the discussion where divergence appeared to cut across the views of Orthodox and Reformed alike, such as a notion of 'the pre-existence' of the Church, or the length to which the Cappadocian distinction between the Energies and the Being of God may be pushed both in theological epistemology and in Pneumatology. It seemed clear that more attention would have to be given to the problems that gave rise to the *filioque* clause in the Western Creed, but that these should be approached through closer attention to the teaching of Athanasius and Cyril of Alexandria with their insistence that everything we say of the Father we must say of the Son except 'Father', and that notions of 'causality' should not be introduced into our understanding of inner-Trinitarian relations or consequently into the way in which the Grace of God incarnate in Jesus Christ is at work in the world. This would involve a deeper and fuller understanding of the element of human participation in divine things as mediated through the humanity of the incarnate Son and Saviour of mankind.

At the conclusion of the general theological discussion on both papers it became evident that a deep consensus among the paticipants had emerged. Dr. Torrance was asked to prepare a short draft which would underline the basic theological direction of all the work accomplished in the three consultations that had taken place, with a view to determining the central content and orientation of the eventual official dialogue which would hopefully be undertaken. This draft was duly presented and led to a substantial discussion on a variety of issues. While continuing to stress the supreme importance of a basic emphasis in future study, centring on the doctrine of the Holy Trinity, the conference specified certain aspects of the Faith that call for further resolution, the relation of the Incarnation to the Creation, the identity of the Church, the interrelation of faith and authority in the Church, the Eucharist and the Ministry, the witness and mission of the Church in life and thought toward the world. Stress was laid upon the fact, however, that, in all of this, thought must proceed from the central understanding of the doctrine of the Triune God. After discussion and amendment, the statement was approved by the group as a whole, entitled, '*Agreed Understanding of the Theological Development and Eventual Direction of Orthodox/Reformed Conversations Leading to Dialogue*'. (The accepted text is printed at the end of this volume.)

Following the adoption of this statement, the consultation turned to procedural matters. It was agreed that sufficient work had now been done, and a significant enough consensus had been reached, for each Delegation to take steps toward asking their appropriate bodies, the Ecumenical Patriarchate and the World Alliance of Reformed Churches, to move into official

dialogue with each other. On the part of the Ecumenical
Patriarchate the proposal would be referred to the Holy Synod
and thereafter to the fourteen autocephalous Orthodox
Churches, and decisions would be communicated to the
Alliance. Likewise the Executive Committee of the World
Alliance of Reformed Churches would communicate its formal
decisions to the Ecumenical Patriarchate. On the assumption
that the results of these moves would be positive, Metropolitan
Chrysostomos indicated what might well take place. From the
Orthodox side a fairly large Commission would need to be
appointed, representing all the Autocephalous Churches. This
would call for a Commission of similar size to be appointed to
represent the Reformed Churches. In that event, he envisaged
that these two Commissions might meet only twice, at the
beginning and at the end of the formal Dialogue, but that the
work would be done by a smaller group of people with possibly
only four from each side, who would keep their parent
Commissions regularly informed of their progress and then
submit a final report, on the ground of which the full
Commissions would make their respective decisions. This
procedure, which had already been outlined at the first
Consultation in Istanbul, was now unanimously endorsed by all
the Orthodox and Reformed representatives.

On the other hand, it seemed advisable for the exploratory
and preparatory consultations to continue. As a result of the
discussions that had taken place, there was a clear convergence
of minds on both sides that particular attention should now be
devoted to the doctrine of the Holy Spirit. Thus an attempt
should be made to clarify the Pneumatological perspective
within which a conjoint understanding of 'one Salvation in
Christ, one Faith, one Church' might eventually be reached, but
within the regulative frame of the doctrine of the Holy Trinity.
It was further recommended in line with agreement on this
proposal that special study should be made of the following
texts: Athanasius, *Letters to Serapion on the Holy Spirit*; Basil, *On the
Holy Spirit*; Gregory Nazianzen, *Theological Oration on the Spirit*;
Calvin, *Institute*, 3.1-2; Karl Barth, *God the Holy Spirit, Church
Dogmatics*, I.1, sect. 12.

In the meantime, however, it was resolved to publish the
theological papers that had been prepared for the three

Consultations in 1979, 1981 and 1983, so that they might be given wider dissemination in the form of a book, in the hope that the discussion they provoked might be of real help to any future dialogue between the Orthodox and Reformed Churches. This task was entrusted to Professor Torrance, who was asked to write an Introduction to the volume which would give an account of the Consultations and thus present the context in which the various documents should be read.

FIRST CONSULTATION

Istanbul

July 26-30, 1979

CHAPTER 1

MEMORANDA ON ORTHODOX/REFORMED RELATIONS

THOMAS F. TORRANCE

Memorandum A

'The Reformed Church' does not set out to be a new or another Church but to be a movement of reform within the One Holy Catholic and Apostolic Church of Jesus Christ, in obedience to its Apostolic foundation in him, and, through constant renewing of the Holy Spirit, seeks throughout its mission on earth steadily to be conformed to Christ as his Body, constantly presenting itself before God through him as a living sacrifice, solely to the glory of God, Father, Son and Holy Spirit. Thus while through the exigencies of history and changing cultures 'Reformed Churches' have arisen, and have taken on an 'autocephalous' character, similar to that of the Orthodox Churches, they are intrinsically committed to the unity of the One Church as the undivided Body of Christ, and continue to seek the realisation of that unity in space and time on the basis of the Apostolic Faith and Practice, which our Lord himself established with the saving economy of his life, death, resurrection and ascension, and with the gift of the Paraclete Spirit who was sent by the Father through him, and by him from the Father, to abide with and to guide the Apostolic Church throughout its earthly mission until he comes again.

The Reformed Church claims to be both 'Apostolic' and 'Catholic' for it does not look to any other foundation than that of the Apostolic Church in what it received from Christ and in his One Spirit and handed on to the world through the Holy Scriptures and through a Ministry dependent on it. The Reformed Church interprets this Apostolic Tradition in agreement with and on the basis of the Catholic theology of the Ecumenical Councils of the undivided Church. The Apostles'

Creed and the Nicene-Constantinopolitan Creed have pre-eminent place in its own faith and doctrine, but in the dogmatic understanding and appropriation of this the Reformed Churches have constantly taken their guidance from the classical Greek Theology, especially as taught by the great Alexandrian and Cappadocian theologians. The Churches which constitute the World Alliance of Reformed Churches have, through their historical and cultural ties in Western Christendom also been deeply influenced by the Augustinian tradition, which is most evident in its understanding of grace in opposition to Pelagianism, in its doctrine of the Church as the Communion of the Elect, and in its conception of Sacrament; but in the doctrine of the Holy Trinity, in Christology, Soteriology and Eschatology they have, with John Calvin, taken their main orientation from the Greek Fathers, and those 'Western' Fathers, Irenaeus and Hilary, who belonged to this Greek tradition.

This orientation marks certain deep differences between the Reformed Churches and the Latin Churches, in Trinitarian theology, in the emphasis upon the Resurrection (the 'caput fidei' as Calvin called it), and in the recovery of the *Epiclesis*, in an understanding of the Church as the Body of Christ, of Baptismal incorporation into him, and of Eucharistic union and communion with him. This is probably most evident in that the epicletic dimension lifts the life, worship and communion of the Reformed Church out of the hard causal and juridical structures of the Latin development which have so deeply characterised Western forms of thought in dogma, law and ecclesiastical institutions. Thus, for example, the Reformed understanding of the 'real presence' is much closer to that of Greek than that of Latin theology. In many respects the Reformed Church stands closest to the Anglican Church in the West, but differs from it in respect of the *Epiclesis* and its bearing upon history, and in that it has always insisted that the order of the Church is basically a *de fide* matter, at which point the 'non-episcopal' character of most Reformed Churches is to be understood. All non-Roman Churches in the West, and especially the Churches in the new world, have been deeply influenced by the notions of 'democracy' that have come out of the 'Protestant' centuries, and not least the nineteenth century, which have affected Church life and practice in a wide way. Yet into this the Reformed Church more than any other Church in the West has constantly asserted the belief that the Church is above all the Body of Christ united to him through his Spirit, that is, in Karl Barth's words, 'Christ's own earthly-historical form of existence, the one Holy Catholic and Apostolic Church', so that throughout history the Church on earth is the provisional representation of the whole world of humanity, called, justified and sanctified in Christ. Moreover, against a democratic understanding of the Ministry, the Reformed Church has always insisted that the ministry is to be understood 'from above and not from below', as deriving from Christ himself the Lord and Head of the Church, and not from the membership of the Church.

The Reformed Church honours the Greek Orthodox Church for its faithfulness to Apostolic Faith and Practice, and to the Catholic theology of the Greek Fathers to which the whole Church of Christ in East and West is so deeply indebted. The Reformed Church also acknowledges that the Orthodox Church has developed a rich Church tradition of worship, life and activity, which transcend the historical and cultural milieu of the Byzantine empire and subsequent developments. It recognises that during this long period forms of piety, personal and monastic, which are distinctive manifestations of the Christian faith, have grown up to become inalienable aspects of ecclesiastical life and essential to the tradition of Orthodox liturgical worship and witness. Some of these forms of piety are strange to the life and witness of the Reformed Churches which have developed in a different cultural and historical milieu and have come to emphasise the word rather than the icon, but Reformed Churches do not regard these differences in forms of piety as entering into the substance of the faith, or as ruling out genuine koinonia between them and the Orthodox Churches. On the other hand, the Reformed Churches appreciate the theological foundations of Orthodox worship and share with the Orthodox the conviction that all earthly forms of worship in the Church are a participation through the Spirit in the on-going worship which the risen and enthroned Christ, the Lamb of God, who is both 'Offerer and Offering', constitutes in his own high-priestly self-presentation before the Father on behalf of all those whom he has redeemed and consecrated in union with himself. They believe that this sharing in the worship of the Father, which Christ himself is, is the heart of the Church's Eucharistic worship and communion, and that it is from that centre that the life and the activity of the Church on earth are nourished and directed.

The Reformed Churches would not wish to enter into discussion with the Orthodox Church without frank admission that there are elements in their own tradition which they must learn to 'unknow' (to borrow a term from the Pseudo-Dionysius), not least in their commitment to unity with other Churches in the One Holy Catholic and Apostolic Church. They believe that it is in ecumenical dialogue and fellowship that this 'unknowing' may take place, as deeper and deeper mutual koinonia in the Mystery of Christ takes place. Hence they enter into discussion ready for critical questions directed at them which may help them to be what they profess to be in their commitment to constant renewal and reformation. With a view to this, it may help at the outset to set out briefly the basic position of the Reformed Churches in respect of the Apostolic Faith and Practice.

The Apostolic Faith

Since the Reformed Churches believe that Apostolicity constitutes the criterion for its understanding of the Oneness, Holiness and Catholicity of the Church, they are committed to the Apostolic Canon of Holy Scripture and to the rule of faith and life which it provides for the Church in all ages. They acknowledge the creeds of the ancient Church, received and formulated by the Nicene Fathers, and accept the doctrinal 'limits' of the great Conciliar statements after Nicaea and Constantinople, especially of Ephesus and Chalcedon. While the Reformed Churches in the sixteenth and seventeenth centuries produced catechetical and confessional formulations for the guidance of their life, teaching and proclamation of the Gospel, these were and are held only as 'secondary standards' subordinate to the Apostolic Faith as mediated through the New Testament, and to the Catholic doctrine as defined by the Apostles' and Nicene-Constantinopolitan Creeds.

Thus the Reformed Churches believe in the Trinity and Unity of the Father, Son and Holy Spirit (the *mia ousia*, the *homoousia*, and *treis hypostaseis*). They are aware of the differing approaches in East and West and of different intepretations of the Unity in relation to the Trinity and of the Trinity in relation to the Unity of God, but do not regard any one of them as an explanation of the Mystery of God's Triunity which is more to be adored than expressed. But they believe that the Trinity and Unity of God is given to us in the Mystery of God's self-communication to his Church in the Incarnation of his Son and in the pouring out of the Holy Spirit.

The Reformed Churches believe in Christ the eternal Son of God who became man for us and our salvation, one undivided Person in two natures. They accept the dogmatic Christological confessions of the Orthodox Ecumenical Councils, and emphasise the vicarious Person and work of Jesus Christ in his birth, life, death, resurrection and ascension, and look for his coming again in great glory to judge and renew the whole creation.

The Reformed Churches believe that the Holy Spirit is God of God, no less than the Father and the Son, and that he proceeds from the Godhead through the Son. While the Reformed Church has traditionally accepted the *Filioque* clause of the Western Creed, by this is not meant that it holds that there are two Sources of the Spirit, or that the *Filioque* explains the hypostatic *idioma* of the Spirit. Rather is it intended to say that the Spirit proceeds from the Father through the Son, and leads us through the Son to the Father, yet in such a way that everything we say of the Father we say of the Son and of the Spirit except 'Father', for the Spirit is not subordinated to the Father or the Son but is of equal honour and being with the Father and the Son in the one indivisible *homoousia*. They believe that the Holy Spirit is at work in the whole creation, sanctifying and bringing it to its true *telos* in God, but that he dwells in the Church in a distinctive way, uniting us to Christ and making us participate in his saving reality, and leading and empowering the Church in the mission on which it has been sent by Christ the Saviour of the world.

Apostolic Practice

The Reformed Church believes that the pattern of its life and mission derives from the pattern which Jesus Christ constituted as the Incarnate Son of God's love in our human existence and nature, and that that pattern is exhibited through the Apostles as the rule of life. That pattern is indivisibly bound up with the Apostolic Ministry which derived immediately from Christ himself, and with the Holy Ministry which the Apostles themselves launched in dependence on their own Apostleship from Christ. The Reformed Church believes that the Holy Ministry thus mediated through the Apostles is the gift of Christ to and for his Church. While the Apostles were the earthly and historical instruments of that mediation, the gift of the Holy Ministry comes in and with the Gift of the Holy Spirit sent upon the Church from the Father, yet in such a way that the gift of the Ministry took its historical shape and order through the practice and ordinances of the Apostles whom Christ set at the head of his Church as its wise 'Masterbuilders'.

The Reformed Church believes that there is only one Priesthood, the Royal Priesthood of Jesus Christ himself, but that through the Spirit the Church as Christ's Body participates in that Priesthood in a distinctive way through serving it in the ministry of Word and Sacrament, and that within the Priesthood of the Church some members are set apart to participate in that priestly service in a particular authoritative way, preaching and acting in Christ's Name and place, in such a way that through their service of him, it is he himself who acts in and through them. The nature of their ministry derives from the servant-form of Jesus Christ the Incarnate and Crucified Son of God, and is thus always a humble and never a lordly form of ministry. This Holy Ministry which cannot be separated from the Word and Mystery of Christ which it ministers is thus of divine origin, character and institution. It does not originate with the Church, but with Christ himself who set it in the Church and makes it efficacious through his own Presence and Spirit, promising it perpetuity and continuity throughout all ages in the building up of the Church and the extension of the Gospel throughout the world until he comes again.

In the historical tradition of the Reformed Churches, attempts were made at the Reformation to re-form the ministry and practice of the Church, which in the culture of Western countries had often become de-formed in such a way as to obscure the true Face of Christ in his Church. But this re-

forming of the ministry and practice of the Church took place —
such was the intention and claim made — in accordance with
the Apostolic Foundation and Pattern of the Church as it was
discerned in the New Testament Scriptures and in the practice
of the Early Church. It became distinctive of the Reformed
Church that *episcope* was held to be lodged not individually in
persons but corporately in the body of Presbyters, i.e., in the
Presbytery as a whole. The 'Bishop' was understood to be the
presiding Presbyter (*Proestos*), while ordination through 'the
laying on of hands by the Presbytery' was mediated from
generation to generation by the *diadoche episkopon/presbuteron* —
that is to say, the Reformed Church sought to take its pattern of
reform from the pattern of the Early Church before the bishop
became separated from the presbytery over which he presided
and attained the character of a 'lordly' figure exercising a
juridical and magisterial function independently of the Presbyters over whom he presided. While in the Western tradition,
theologically there was held to be no higher 'order' than that of
the Presbyter, who was ordained 'in order to the Eucharist', so
that the Bishop was not held to be superior in order but only in
jurisdiction, actually the Bishop became invested by canon law
with princely powers so that he came to exercise a lordly
function in his own independent right. Since that practice had
given rise to so much worldliness and abuse in the Western
Church, the Reformers sought to recover the 'servant form' of
the ministry after the pattern of 'the Servant Form of Christ
himself', and the humble, evangelical form of the early Church
Bishop who did not lord it over the Eucharist but served Christ
in the Eucharist as a steward of the mysteries of God.

In this way the Reformed Church came to operate with a
twofold pattern of ministry: that of the presbyter or bishop who
dispenses the mysteries of God in Word and Sacrament, and
that of the elder or deacon who prompts the congregation or
people to receive the mysteries of God in Word and Sacrament.
Each local Church has a council of these elder-deacons, presided
over by the Presbyter-Bishops, after the pattern of the
Eucharistic celebration in the Early Church. The local Councils
of Churches are subordinate to the Presbytery which comprises
all the ordained Presbyters and one representative from the
elder-deacons, but the Presbytery has its own elected President

known as the 'Moderator'. This Presbytery is recognised as a 'sacral court' having magisterial function, but in its turn it is subordinate along with other Presbyteries to a General Assembly, similarly comprised, which is presided over by its 'Moderator'. The national Reformed Churches are autocephalous like Orthodox Churches. But all the Reformed Churches are united through common Apostolic Faith and Practice (as they understand it), in a world-wide union known as 'The Alliance of Reformed Churches', in which, however, there are no special prerogatives of seniority, as in the Orthodox Church, and which constitutes no more than a *Communion* or Family of Reformed Churches. It is not claimed by the Reformed Churches that their order is derived from some Biblical 'blueprint', but only that it is 'agreeable to the Word of God', as they interpret the New Testament in the light of the Apostolic and early Catholic tradition, and that it is always open to revision and re-form in obedience to Jesus Christ and the Apostolic Foundation of the Church in him. The Reformed Churches have, therefore, a rather open outlook (perhaps more open than the Anglican and the Lutheran in certain respects) and it is this character they seek to maintain in all ecumenical discussion and all proposals for intercommunion or Church union. It is the theological foundation for Church life and order that is important for them, which requires Church law to be subordinated to the Gospel so that it may be used only to serve the rule of Christ and his Spirit in the Church.

There are clearly differences in ethos, practice and order between the Reformed and the Orthodox Churches, but the agreement in basic theology would appear to be deeply grounded. Hence it would seem best for serious discussions between the Orthodox and the Reformed to concern themselves with these fundamental issues in doctrine and from an agreement or consensus there to carry the discussion into the areas of Church, Ministry and Sacraments where divergences are most apparent.

In this case, it would be most helpful if discussions began with the doctrine of the *Holy Trinity*: and then moved from there into the doctrines of *the Son* and *the Spirit*, and then to the doctrine of *the Eucharist*. That would provide the right context for discussion about *the Church and the Ministry*. The conversations could aim at a clarification of the understanding which East and West, in this case the Orthodox and the Reformed, have of their common foundation in the Alexandrian and Cappadocian theology, to which the Conciliar Statements are so heavily indebted. At first glance it is suggested that deepest agreement could be reached on the basis of the Athanasian-Cyrilline theology, which is impeccably Orthodox, and which is so basic to the Reformed Church. The Cappadocian theology also deeply influenced the Reformed Church, not least through John Calvin, whose teaching was so indebted to and so close to that of St. Gregory Nazianzen that he was given the title 'ho theologos' by Philip Melanchthon. The Athanasian-Cyrilline theology carries a deeper grasp of the Vicarious Humanity of Christ which is of special significance for the Reformed, as also for the modern liturgical renewal, in which we are all engaged in some measure. It may well be the case that by approaching the doctrine of the Trinity in this way, we could cut behind the difference between East and West over the 'Filioque' clause, and establish full and deep agreement on the doctrine of the Holy Spirit as well as the doctrine of the Son — not least if we followed the Cappadocians (cf. Nazianzen's Fifth Oration on the Spirit), Hilary of Poitiers, and Calvin, in the 'apophatic' reserve they maintained in handling the 'images' used in elucidation of the Trinitarian relations in God.

From this basis it may be possible to cut behind the damaging dualism that separated the traditional 'Antiochene' and 'Alexandrian' approaches to Christology and Soteriology, affecting the understanding of the Priesthood of Christ, and consequently of 'priesthood' in the Church and the Liturgy; but from this basis also it may be possible to cut behind the divergences not only between East and West but between the 'Chalcedonian' and 'non-Chalcedonian' positions in the East, which, it is now evident, have to do with deep epistemological and cosmological dualisms which have left their mark on later Byzantine thought in the East and Augustinian thought in the West. Further, this line of approach opens up classical Greek theology to fresh appreciation in the context of the modern scientific world, as that theology which is the most relevant of all for our modern scientific world, in its rejection of the ancient, mediaeval and modern dualisms, and in recovering the unitary understanding of the created universe so deeply embedded especially in the great Alexandrian understanding of the Incarnation and Creation. One steady effect of such a clarification would be the sifting clear of the central and basic Christian convictions from pseudo-theological and obsolete scientific notions derived from time-conditioned notions of a past culture. Out of this would emerge, in a deeper way than East/West or Roman Catholic/Evangelical Churches have been able to achieve so far, a common basis for agreement on the questions of authority in the Church and in the formulation and development of Christian doctrine, and if we can reach a deeper Trinitarian understanding of the creation, a common basis also for the relation between Christian Faith and the modern scientific world. It would appear that modern scientific understanding of the created universe which cuts away the old damaging dualisms of the past can help us to bridge the gap between *icon* and *word*, for example, which is so symptomatic of the divergence between the Orthodox and the Reformed.

Memorandum B

Obviously in the ecumenical context, discussions on the Church, Ministry and Sacraments will have to take place. Certainly Reformed theology is well based for this, because of the work of Calvin, and of its classical 'de fide' understanding of these doctrines. Calvin was the first in the West to break with the Augustinian/Thomist dualist notion of the Church as body/soul (which yielded the dualism between legal institution and 'mystical body'), and the first really to give an adequate *theological* account of the Church as the Body of Christ in history, and thus to link the doctrine of the Church profoundly with the doctrine of Christ, the incarnate Son of God. (Calvin was here partially followed by the Tridentine Catechism, but that more realist and Christological conception of the Church remained abortive until Vatican II). At the same time Calvin was the first theologian in the West after Hilary (with the partial exception of St. Anselm) to lay the basis for a more adequate doctrine of the Holy Spirit, which is closely linked to the doctrine of Christ. Again, Calvin was the only one of the Reformers who broke with the Boethian/Thomist 'individualist' notion of 'person'. Here he follows in the tradition of Hilary of Poitiers and Richard of St. Victor (as well as Athanasius and Cyril of Alexandria), whose doctrine of the Trinity is the nearest in the West to the classical position of the Greek Church. These doctrines stand behind Calvin's understanding of the Church and Sacraments. Here another point of primary importance must be noted: Calvin's radical break with the Roman and Lutheran notion of 'space' or 'place' (determined by Aristotle's conceptions in the fourth book of his *Physics*), in which he followed closely the teaching of the Greek Fathers, Athanasius, Nazianzen, Nyssa and Cyril of Alexandria. It is at this point that divergences in the understanding of the Incarnation and the Real Presence arise between Calvin and the Latin tradition, which again throws Calvin's theology into the Eastern type.

There are, of course, problems in Calvin's theology, to which we must not shut our eyes. The most obvious relates to his doctrine of predestination with its apparent split in the doctrine of God, which gives a 'Nestorian' appearance: that is, a duality between the eternal God as he is in himself, and God as he manifests himself in his incarnate and redemptive form in Jesus Christ. The strange thing is that Calvin does not follow the Latins (apart from Irenaeus and Hilary, who were really 'Greek' in their outlook and theology) in his Christology and Soteriology, but Athanasius and Cyril of Alexandria; so that this element of 'Nestorianism' does not derive from his Christology as such (although we should bear in mind the Scotist reaction against Thomist 'Eutychianism', mediated to Calvin through John Major along with his doctrine of the Trinity). Calvin learned from Cyril of Alexandria (specifically from Oecolampadius' Latin edition of Cyril's works) the enormous emphasis, which he made his own (including Cyril's vocabulary) on the servant obedience of the incarnate Son, which is so characteristic of the Reformed doctrine of Christ and Salvation. How then did the 'Nestorian' dualism in his doctrine of God come into Calvin's thought? Evidently it came partly from Augustine, to whom he was indebted for much of his doctrine of predestination, but also from the influence of Antiochene exegetes upon him, notably St. Chrysostom, reinforced by Calvin's openness to Jewish OT scholarship. But perhaps the decisive thing here is that he was influenced by the distinction

begun by the Cappadocians between the eternal 'Being' of God
and his 'Energies' (Calvin's thought stood so close to Nazianzen
that Melanchthon actually transferred to Calvin the title the
ancients gave to Nazianzen, 'ho theologos'). It was, alas, that
dualism, backed by a resurrected Origenism and by Neoplatonic influence, which led Byzantine thought into a dualist
outlook basically similar to the Augustinian. It would seem to
me that at some time the ultimate doctrine of God behind
Christology would require to be looked at, if we are to enter into
any basic and fruitful discussions with the Orthodox. This
could, in my view, be done best by reference to the teaching of
St. Athanasius.

The Orthodox Church has problems of its own, which are
deeper than most Orthodox theologians realise, and which may
be summarised briefly by saying that its theology has tended in
recent centuries (but going back to the post-Chalcedonian
period) to rest upon the Cappadocian rather than upon the
Athanasian-Cyrilline axis. It was owing to the Cappadocian
basis, e.g. its tendency toward the double notion of 'substance', a
generic and a particular (which was deepened by the Dionysian
and Neoplatonic developments together with the revival of
Aristotelian thought in the schools from Byzantium to Gaza),
that Greek theology became trapped in a position in which those
post-Chalcedonians who were opposed to dualism and who
resented the Latin/Leonine interpretation of Chalcedon were
denigrated as 'monophysite' heretics — a disastrous misunderstanding which resulted in the schism of the Copts from the
Byzantines. The Copts and other 'non-Chalcedonians', were
not really monophysite, for they grounded their theology very
rigorously on Cyril of Alexandria, as is evident, for example, in
the physics of John Philoponos of Alexandria (not to be confused
with 'John the Grammarian'). The rejection by the Greek
Orthodox, now Byzantine, of these 'non-Chalcedonians', had
the effect of deepening the dualism in their own thought, in
which they were prone, with emphasis upon the apophatic side
of that dualism, to oppose the Latins with their emphasis on the
cataphatic side of the same dualism.

These are problems that require to be solved, if deep
ecumenical relations are to be achieved. The modern Greek
Orthodox have already taken considerable steps in this

direction, largely through Methodios of Aksum (now of Thyateira and Great Britain), in respect of the difference between the 'Chalcedonians' and 'non-Chalcedonians' (especially the Coptic, Ethiopic and Syrian Christians), which augurs well for their discussions with us. The depth of the problem we face in the West can be seen from the decisively Latin and distorted Leonine and Augustinian slant given to the interpretation of the Greek Fathers one finds in such a work as that of the great Grillmeier, almost wholly uncritically accepted by Western scholars!

It would seem to me in view of all this that a deep-going dialogue on the most fundamental issues between the Reformed and the Orthodox would serve the whole Faith and Order work of the Ecumenical movement, and lay a sounder basis for agreement and unity in the area of Church, Ministry and Sacraments.

My proposal, therefore, which I have already outlined to the Greek Orthodox Patriarchs and Archbishops in the Middle East, is that our discussions should begin with the doctrine of the *Holy Trinity*; and move from there into the doctrines of the Son and the Spirit, and then into the doctrines of the Eucharist and the Church and the Ministry (probably in that order). The basic question I would set down for this discussion would be whether there is not a far-reaching difference between the teaching of Athanasius and Cyril on the one hand and that of the Cappadocians on the other hand. The problem is sharpest at the point where the Cappadocians speak of God the Father unreservedly in terms of *aitia*, *pege* and *arche*, but not of the Son or of the Spirit, whereas Athanasius' great principle ran that we say of the Son everything we say of the Father, except 'Father'. Bound up with this difference is the fact that the Cappadocians formalised the meaning of the terms '*ousia*' and '*hypostasis*' in the formula: '*One ousia, three hypostaseis*', thereby moving in an Aristotelian direction, whereas for Athanasius the use of these terms does not depend on any formal defining of them but on that to which they refer and by which their meaning is wholly governed — which represents a more elastic and dynamic use of theological terms. The danger of the Cappadocian position was pointed out by Cyril of Alexandria in protesting against the use of *aitia* of intra-Trinitarian relations. The Cappadocians were in a difficulty, for their formula could easily lead into an apparently 'tritheist' position, since they tended to use '*ousia*' in a generic and not in a concrete sense; consequently they had to defend themselves against such a charge and did so (see especially Nyssa's work 'That There are not Three Gods'). But they did so at the expense of a distinction between the Deity of the Father as wholly underived, 'uncaused' Deity, and the Deity of the Son and of the Spirit as eternally 'caused' or derived. At the same time, this led to the tendency to identify 'Father' = the Godhead with 'Father' = the Person of the Father. It was, in my view, this Cappadocian distinction that provided the ground for the problem of the understanding of the procession of the Spirit when East and West split over the notorious '*filioque*' clause added by the West to the Nicene-Constantinopolitan Creed, without the authority of an Ecumenical Council, and the Greeks responded by insisting on the procession of the Spirit from 'the Father *only*' which implied 'from the *Person* of the Father'. If the Son and the Spirit are eternally 'caused' by the Father, how can it be said that the Spirit proceeds from the Son so described? But if the Spirit does not proceed from the Son as well as the Father, then, for the West, that would import a damage to belief in the unqualified Deity of the Son. Moreover the problem arose on both sides of whether the One God that is the Godhead can be thought of as 'Person', or whether 'Person' is to be restricted to the three 'Persons' of the Father, the Son and the Spirit. For the Greeks that difficulty was not so acute as for the Latins, since the Greek formula 'from the Father only' identified the 'Father' with the 'Person of the Father'. Other questions enter into this '*filioque*' dispute, with some right and some wrong on both sides, but the basic difficulty which ought not to have arisen comes from the Cappadocian distinction in the Trinity — which is, incidentally, allied at a second-order level to their distinction between the 'Being' of God and his 'Energies'. I would maintain that had the Greek Church remained steadfast to the Athanasian-Cyrilline basis, the whole problem, and the division that followed it, would probably not have risen: nor would the Greeks have lapsed into their characteristic Byzantine dualism. In other words, by returning to the impeccably Orthodox and non-dualist basis of Athanasius and Cyril we ought to be able to cut behind the schism between East and West over the '*filioque*', and at the same time provide a deeper basis for the healing of the rift between Evangelical and Catholic wings of the Church, not to mention the rift between the Orthodox and the so-called 'Monophysite' Churches.

I believe that if we can agree on a basic doctrine of the Trinity, which must be far nearer to the traditional doctrine of the East and West (cf. '*An Ecumenical Consensus on the Doctrine of the Trinity*' prepared by the Académie Internationale des Sciences Religieuses), and we can go on to clear up problems regarding Christology, cut behind the damaging dualism which severs theology into 'Antiochene' and 'Alexandrian' camps, with unfortunate effects in the liturgy as well. For example, the Byzantine liturgy through Chrysostom's influence has taken on dualist Antiochene elements, evident not least in the notion of the Priesthood of Christ and the priesthood of the Church — cf. here the Commentary on the Liturgy by Nicholas Cabasilas. But we must also deal especially with the insidious effect of the Aristotelian doctrine of space/place, reintroduced into the Greek Church, against the Athanasians, Cappadocians, and Cyrillians, by John of Damascus, with serious problems in Christology and even in the doctrine of the Trinity, not to mention epistemology and cosmology. Thus I believe we could more or less settle certain basic issues in Christology — which cannot but help East and West, and which would cut behind those divergences in the doctrine of the Eucharist and the Ministry which are related to the doctrines of Grace, the Real Presence, Sacrifice, etc., but also to the concept of the continuity of the Church and its Ministry in the Eucharistic Life of the People of God. Far from weakening the notion of the real presence of the risen Christ in the Church and the Sacraments, and far from damaging the notions of continuity and dynamic stability of the ministry throughout history, this can only deepen and strengthen them.

Finally, I would argue that this line of approach opens up classical Greek theology to fresh appreciation in the context of the modern scientific world, which makes it clear that that theology is the most relevant of all for our modern scientific world, as well as for the union of the whole Church in Christ today. One steady effect it has is to help us to cleanse our thought of pseudo-theological concepts which are little more than passing, time-conditioned notions derived from an obsolete culture that have, unfortunately, been given the sanction of ecclesiastical authority in the past. Out of this there would naturally emerge, in a deeper way than the East/West or Roman Catholic/Evangelical Churches have been able to treat of it so far, the problem of *authority* in the formulation and development of Christian doctrine. I see no reason why we should not at this tricky point also come to a closer agreement than has hitherto been possible in the traditional patterns of ecumenical discussion, in which we begin from the wrong end. But it would involve a radical rethinking of the basis of canon law, which in West and East, has taken into itself (e.g., through Leo the Great and Justinian) the dualist orientation of Stoic legal thought. This could be undermined with considerable effectiveness by reference to the non-dualist notions of physical law which we see already in John Philoponos and now in the post-Einsteinian non-dualist understanding of the created order. This would have immense benefit for the Roman Catholic Church in the impasse in which they find themselves with respect to the projected *Lex Fundamentalis Ecclesiae*, but also for the Orthodox, who not only behind the Iron Curtain but in the Middle East and Ethiopia have to face the problems posed by Marxist thought. The latter will clearly be of increasing significance for the Orthodox Church in Muslim countries. To reach any really significant fruit in this direction we would have to develop, as the Church has not yet done, a *Trinitarian understanding of the creation.*

SECOND CONSULTATION

Geneva

February 15-18, 1981

CHAPTER 2

GOD'S IMMUTABILITY AND COMMUNICABILITY

EMILIANOS TIMIADIS

Preamble

While the Triune God remains the very centre of our faith the early Fathers were confronted with further consequent problems. The ongoing process of doctrinal formulation dealt with the relationship in the Trinity and above all the distinction between God's essence and the divine energies. In doing this they often borrowed terms from existing rich, Platonic, philosophical language and analogies. They could not do otherwise, since such terms were excellent vehicles conveying in the best way the mystery of our faith. Thus we find a continuity of Patristic thought in explaining God's communicability to man in full harmony with God's immutability. It has been suggested that if the Church had stayed with the Athanasian-Cyrillian Christological formula, no division would have been produced by the so-called pre-Chalcedonians, and the Byzantines would not have lapsed into their 'dualism'. Such an accusation is exaggerated, for the simple reason that the Church does not regard theological formulations as petrified sentences, excluding any new re-interpretation and the introduction of more acceptable terms. The Fathers on the contrary were always trying to find the language of their time, without absolutising terms and words. Thus we can see a certain harmony among them, as they express in different terms the same truth or doctrine. Thus we have the *Consensus Patrum*.

Over against a misconception of inactive *ousia* the doctrine of God as Person was underlined and explained. God is continuously in action, working out our salvation. He is not giving something, but himself, coming to meet each one of us. We have an encounter between Person and person. And yet we wonder at the mystery of a God who at the same time is known and unknown, accessible and inaccessible.

What therefore are the areas of Trinitarian research among the Fathers? What is the bearing of Christ's Incarnation on the redeemed people? The Covenant relation is, no doubt, of paramount importance for such investigations. Because he is love, he overcomes the limitations of time and space.

God is not utterly inexpressible. He is a self-naming God, that is, a God naming his own being, while we, from a human point of view, attribute to God a variety of names. This constitutes another area of the Fathers' concern. Something happens in history. We encounter an action (δρώμενον) and a principal everlasting actor (δρῶν). God ontologically penetrates history. He is communicable (*methektos*). The outgoing of grace shows his continuous *philanthropia* for mankind. The Fathers arrived not at Hellenized Christianity but a Christianised Hellenism. They made an understandable synthesis by a blend of Jewish-Hellenic-Christian conceptions and terminology. God's economy was never discontinued. The Church of the OT continues in the NT.

This personal *koinonia* takes place above all in the Church and through the saving mysteries. The Triune God who transcends time and space, becomes through the divine energies one with us, one body. This oneness is seen during the *Epiklesis*, the Eucharist being the climax of such a communion. Thus the Trinitarian economy is not static but active, saving, restoring, freeing and appealing to man for acceptance and for sonship. This leads to the doctrine of *Theosis*.

Patristic theology in general underlines the organic synthesis between God's transcendence and his reality in creation and history, referring to these uncreated energies which flow from God's presence. This relationship makes for real and constant human participation in the divine mystery. The Holy Trinity is not only the mystery of a living and personal God, but also the mystery of God in communion. This central place of *methexis* serves to avoid a naturalistic and personalistic view of divine nature. The Trinity is the origin and very model of the unity of the Church, of mankind and of the individual person. This living, personal and coinherent Trinity is not a nominal image, but the revelation of the divine reality.

With these schematic paragraphs we have a summary of the present essay reflecting the Orthodox view on a vital issue, relevant to the forthcoming theological dialogue with the Reformed Churches.

An introduction to the Patristic method

The student of Trinitarian Theology in depth is inevitably baffled at certain points. His thirst and effort for a better understanding of the mystery of the Triune God is never satisfied. All our faith formulated so solidly by the Fathers and reconfirmed by the Ecumenical Councils still provokes wonder and open questions, such as those summarised by Professor Torrance in an honest and scholarly way. This paper does not intend to answer all of them. Simply, because of the limitations imposed, it seeks to explain the spectrum of Trinitarian Theology by merely touching, in the process of developing arguments, on a few points emerging from Torrance's paper.

In saying this, I feel that questions and answers are intermingled in our classical theology. What we hope to find as an answer in an expected place, is to be found, surprisingly, not there, but elsewhere. When Athanasius of Alexandria or Basil of Caesarea set out to speak of the Spirit, they touch on a great variety of subjects: soteriology or Christology, distinguishing between 'being' (*ousia*) and 'energies' (*energeiai*), without neglecting other items which matters, implicitly or explicitly may be of immediate interest, thereby enriching and sustaining their expositions. The present-day reader will be disappointed if he looks for clear-cut statements and neatly measured definitions. This is not the method of Patristics. Language, of course, constitutes another main difficulty. The same word by the same ecclesiastical doctor can be found in different places with different connotations and meaning. For them, terminology is not an absolute, an end in itself. It is, rather, an instrument, a tool in their effort to make the content of our faith more meaningful, to fight errors, to instruct catechumens, to strengthen the weak in faith.

Of course, they draw considerable edifying material, both spiritual and secular, from Greek philosophy; where necessary, they use metaphors, even their own analogies and imagery in a comparative method. They are conscious that a Christian listener or reader stands to benefit from this 'phenomenology' or philological semantics, rendered fertile by the *spermatikos logos*. Without being grammarians, copyists or plagiarists, they are children of their times, of their cultural and linguistic milieu. The opposite would have been disastrous, had they ignored or fanatically hated every beautiful and positive value outside the Church.

We risk betraying the real thought and intention of the Fathers if, with our contemporary pre-conceived views, after fifteen centuries, we try to give our own interpretation of some of their linguistic expressions and conceptions. This is the case of terms frequently met with in their writings: οὐσία, ἐνέργεια, διάστημα, πρόσωπον, γέννησις versus γένεσις, αἰτία, πηγή, ἀρχή, the Holy Spirit's real place in the cosmos and in the daily life of the Church, the coinherent action of the Three Persons, or the Trinitarian Economy. It needs a certain expertise to penetrate into the inner world and thinking of the Fathers and to discern a variety of issues from a truly patristic angle.

Any contemporary theological investigation loses considerably if issues are isolated, detached from their whole historical and intellectual contest. There is an interrelation of mutual complementarity between all theological questions. It is time that, instead of a fragmentary and partial approach, we began to think and study such important issues in a holistic way, in a 'catholic' way, ecumenically, contextually, taking a wide range of issues together, complementing what is partial and missing in one with other elements found scattered here and there. Nobody knows the limits and the boundaries of dogma. Its dimensions can be grasped only by one versed in Patristics and living an ascetic and liturgical spirituality.

It is unfair, again, to introduce irrelevant questions, ἀδιάφορα or θεολογούμενα into the sifting process of Patristics. The Fathers were fully aware of most of the criticisms which might be levelled at them today, or by the generations to come. Through their sensibility and prophetic vision they were easily able to foresee in their opponents the hidden dangers for the Church and for mankind both in their time and later. They could easily compromise with positions viewed as moderate and harmless, but they were persistent and adamant when the whole of the

Faith was at stake. Truth is indivisible. A small part, distorted, will sooner or later contaminate the rest. In matters of faith there is no room for bargaining. There were certainly moments of wavering between silence and courageous speech. Thus, on the divinity of the Holy Spirit, we see hesitation upon hesitation. Finally, Gregory of Nazianzus clearly and formally stated the divinity of the Holy Spirit by asking: 'How long shall we still place the light under a bushel and withhold the perfect Divinity from others?' (*Oratio* 12, 6).

* * *

All those who firmly believe in a Supreme Being legitimately also ask: Who is our God? We believe that *he is*, *he exists*. But in what does his existence consist? What does he do? How does he behave? Is he separated completely from the world of creation, self-centred, living in self-admiring beatitude, or does he turn to help his creation, and, if so, how?

This difficulty confronted even the earliest iconographers. There is not a trace of any attempt to depict God the Father found in the catacombs. Instead, we find the typology of Abraham's hospitality towards the three Angels, or the mysterious Burning Bush with the enigmatic inscription: 'I am that I am'. The unfortunate caricatured figure of an old man representing our Father-God in heaven is of very late origin.

In investigating God's relationship with the creation, certain fundamental questions emerge. These pages will provide a brief survey of them from the Orthodox angle. By speaking of God's very essence as *ousia*, immutable and everlasting, the Alexandrian and Cappadocian Fathers provided a secure basis for defining God's nature, whilst characterising his active interest in the creation in the form of divine 'energies'. The two being concomitant, one cannot accuse the early Fathers of dualism on account of their having borrowed terms from Greek philosophers and notably Aristotle.

God's activity

The early Church was fully conscious of the difficulties inherent in using human terms to describe God's actual Being. While Christian teachers were agreed about God's unchangeability, intemporality, immateriality, immutability and eternity, they nevertheless asked: how does such a God move, act, deal with this creation? Wrongly the Fathers were accused of being too 'apophatic'. On the contrary, they tried to deepen their knowledge of the mystery of the Godhead and revealed truth of the Triune God's economy. But soon they understood the limits of theological research and investigation; they were at certain points 'cataphatic', but at others inevitably 'apophatic'. It would be unfair to absolutise the methods used, apophatic or cataphatic, by exalting the one over the other. Both have their place, both were applied according to need. Aware that such an endeavour was not a mere intellectual exercise but a matter of faith, they pursued their studies in fear and prayer. Pseudo-Denys the Areopagite, from the very first lines of his *Mystical Theology*, invokes the help of the Holy Trinity, seeking illumination, so that the ineffable and infinite mysteries of theology may be revealed, for they are covered by *agnosia*, a cloud of silence and mystery (*PG* 3, 997).

To man, however, is given the privilege of penetrating into the mystery of a Triune God. Although he is a fallen creature, deformed and finite, he can attain to the notion that God exists, either through the surrounding creation or knowledge in faith. We can obtain a certain *Theognosia* (Basil: *Letters* 233 and 235; *PG* 32, 872). What God really is, is and will remain beyond our capacities. But how he comes into contact with the creation, this can be known through his activities (Cyril of Alexandria: *Con. Julianum* 3; *PG* 76, 653). Origen, too, was deeply preoccupied with this mystery. From God's immutability, he goes further, stressing his active presence and intervention through providence and economy in the world's destiny. Thus he refutes the pagan thinkers, who, like Plato, refused any idea of communication of the divine with the human, for the simple reason that humans are inferior beings, incompatible with God's majesty. A certain determinism or fatalism is inevitable, they claimed, and this view has been reflected throughout history in a humanistic context.

Origen in this respect detects a God of *philanthropia* in the mystery of the risen Christ, with all the qualities of a *person* who is ready to love, to intervene, to help, to succour, to protect, to save, to redeem. The Christian God certainly remains immutable in his essence, but at the same time he is living, active, saving, offering his hand to sustain his created beings. In answering the deterministic approach of Celsus, Origen further develops this predominant idea of God's *energeia* and *oikonomia* (*Contra Celsum* 4, 14).

Again, while these Fathers succeeded in finding an appropriate language to describe God's attributes, they also warned us that any term is but poor and inadequate, relative and approximate through being human, and as such cannot convey the whole truth. Their frequent use of the controversial term '*ousia*' does not designate an absolute. They make it clear that God is, in fact, 'beyond *ousia*' = ὑπερούσιος (Denys: *Mystical Theology*; *PG* 3, 1048), πάσης οὐσίας ἐπέκεινα (*De div. Nomin.* I; *PG* 3, 588). Words and terms are borrowed from our earthly experience and daily events. They have but a relative value, offering only analogies, which scarcely correspond to the ultimate reality. One of the earliest hymns of Jesus' Nativity says that 'The Virgin gives birth today to Him who surpasses all essence' (*hyperousios*): "Η Παρθένος σήμερον τὸν ὑπερούσιον τίκτει'.

Origen was writing during a critical transitional period of history. The world situation was such, that many were wondering whether faith in the absolute sovereignty of God could have any meaning. Society was in a state of decomposition and seething unrest. Quite apart from 'natural' calamities, such as flood and famine, etc., there was the appalling carnage of warfare. But for the Fathers, as for Origen, it did not follow that God had lost control of the world or that he remained indifferent to its fate. Nor did it follow that he was either powerless or unwilling to intervene and set things right. The fault, as Cassius admonished Brutus, is not in heaven above but in our distorted picture of God. In suppressing the truth about God, man simultaneously suppressed the truth about himself. To deny an active God is to deny one's own creatureliness and meaningful place in the cosmos. And this in turn is to deny the true meaning of man's existence, because only in his creaturely relationship to his Creator, can he realise the purpose and integrity of his being. Such is the way in which Gregory of Nyssa aproaches the difficulties of theological terminology. What prevails is *agnosia*, but not agnosticism (*Not Three Gods*; *PG* 45, 121).

Perhaps the first honestly to dare to reject all the current 'names' of God was Denys the Areopagite, in which he was partly right and partly wrong: 'The divine is neither a word nor a notion; it cannot be spoken of, thought of, is not number, is not order, is not size, is not equality, not quantity or light. It does not "live", is not light, is not essence' (*Mystical Theology* 5; *PG* 3, 1045). In view of such a negative attitude, man could easily fall into despair and even atheism. How, then, was he to go on to ask what is and what is not God?

The answer, as expected, was not given by man but by God himself. He has, in fact, revealed to the creatures the true *Theologia*. God can certainly be conceived of from the harmony and beauty of the created things, says the book of Wisdom (13:5). The heavens give an account of God's glory and the firmament shows forth his handiwork. Day unto day utters speech, and night unto night shows knowledge (Ps. 19:2-3). Of course the creation, for the man of good faith, offers many evidences of God's existence. But the problem lies elsewhere. *Who* is the living God, for he is not as we are? Can we know him, even incompletely?

It seems that most of the Fathers were inclined to a doxological approach to the Divine Being, as one to be worshipped and contemplated rather than described. Because of the human inability to find appropriate names for God's nature, the more his majesty was eminent, the more man was moved to praise and worship what he was unable to define (Gregory of Nyssa, *Contra Eunom.* 10; *PG* 45, 1108). Basil of Caesarea also admitted that his ultimate being (*ousia*) was ineffable, invisible to all, incomprehensible, inexpressible: 'Τὴν οὐσίαν ἀπερίοπτον εἶναι παντὶ ... ἄρρητος παντελῶς ἡ οὐσία τοῦ θεοῦ' (*Contra Eunom.* 1, 13-14; *PG* 29, 544).

Frankly speaking, the Fathers found themselves in an impossible situation, perplexed as to how to approach this unique and unparalleled subject of ultimate Being. Their intelligence and eagerness for research were no less than ours. Whilst using the most appropriate terms human language could afford, they were not completely happy with them. Their bewilderment is honestly confessed throughout their writings. Gregory of Nyssa sees the term θεός as conveying only a part of its whole meaning to us; for did not Saint Paul himself say: 'His name surpasses every other name' (Phil. 2:9)? The fact that he surpasses all human perception and remains beyond all denomination (ὀνομαστικὴ περίληψις) is proof of his inaccessibility and ineffable creative majesty (*Contra Eunom.* 10; *PG* 45, 1108). The subject before us, says Cyril of Alexandria, is so paradoxical, a-temporal, immaterial, so beyond qualification, description, analysis, categorisation and formulation (*Contra Anthropomorphites* 4; *PG* 76, 1084). No name borrowed from human language, even the most eloquent and sophisticated, can describe God's actual nature. This is the reason why several names are often used together to suggest one single attribute of God.

Of course there is unlimited freedom for further inquiry into God's identity. The more mystery covers the Divinity, the more man is attracted to it, seeking to unveil it by the force of his intellect. Faced with the deep cloud of incomprehensibility covering the Deity, the Fathers, from the apologists Athenagoras and Irenaeus on, although involved in the Christological conflicts, spent a lot of their time developing the doctrine distinguishing the divine '*ousia*' from its 'energies'. John Chrysostom refers to such a dilemma commenting on the vision of the Prophet Isaiah (Is. 6), seeing Yahweh sitting on a high throne and the Seraphim surrounding him with faces and feet covered by their wings: 'Why do they cover their faces and put forward their wings? Because they could not bear the brightness coming from the throne and the light, although the angels did not see that light itself, or the infinite essence, but only such visible things which constituted a condescension. What then is this condescension (*synkatabasis*)? When God is seen by us not precisely as such, but as far as one is able to see him, he shows himself in such a way as to respond to the weakness of those seeking to see him … therefore, when the prophet says "I saw the Lord", he did not see in reality the essence of God, but only this condescension' (*On Incomprehensibility* 3, 3; *PG* 48, 722).

The originality of Patristic usage

Once language penetrates into theology, it influences it to such a degree that it often becomes more important than the subject itself. It may provoke controversies, polemics, sterile dialectical conflicts. Thus it shows its strength but also its weakness. It may prevent flexibility, free expression in theological thinking, violating its mandate by absolutising religious formulae. Instead of being considered as a manageable instrument for formulation and even reformulation when necessary, it remains fettered to immovable, monolithic, terms. Disaster upon disaster has been accumulated in Church history arising from semantics and theological expressions. This was not because behind the terms used there were not hidden other issues too, but because an unbalanced confidence in words used to describe God's nature showed ignorance of the relativity of human language and ignorance of the very mystery of God. Words should serve faith and not the opposite.

Such was the answer of the Chalcedonians with regard to the revised Christology of the followers of the Ephesian Formula, in refusing any new wording. Their weakness consisted in sacralising terminology, in place of the earlier adoration beyond words. Hence Pseudo-Denys reacted to quarrels about names aiming at the imprisonment of the Divinity in words. Seeing the endless parade of pretentious terms concerning God, he rejected them out of fear that they simply spoke *about* God rather than *of* God (*De divin. nom.* 7; *PG* 3, 872; cf. Maximus the Confessor: *Scholia in divin. nom.*; *PG* 4, 189, 204, 253). It seems, indeed, that this conflict is inherent in human nature: to adore and yet to domesticate the Creator, to locate him in narrow definitions or categories evolved from our own mind. And when one arrives at an impasse because of the human poverty of expression, one is prompted to remember that God is Spirit. Of course, a minimum of formulation is needed, but always with the understanding that it has indicative character pointing to further meditation and theological reflection.

The Fathers were conscious of the philosophical origin of most of the Christological terms being used for the formulation of this mystery; therefore they tried to Christianise the terminology. One of the difficulties before them was the abundance of nuances: such is the case with *ousia* and *hypostasis*, which provoked a battle lasting many centuries. The same happened with *hypostasis* and *prosopon*, etc. Thus Epiphanius of Cyprus (*Libr. Haer.* 69, 70; *PG* 42, 317) and Athanasius of Alexandria (*Decr. Nicaean. Concil.* 27; *PG* 25, 465), considered *ousia* and *hypostasis* as almost identical. Even the 1st Ecumenical Council considered them as equivalent, as can be seen in the anathema added to the Nicene Creed, in which all are condemned who teach that the Son is of another *hypostasis* or essence. The confusion was increased by the provincial translation from Greek into Latin, which rendered *hypostasis* — divine being — as *substantia*. To the Cappadocian Fathers is attributed the merit of having made every effort to establish the distinction between *ousia* and *hypostasis* on the one hand, and on the other to offer a justified preference for *hypostasis* as against *prosopon*.

The process of establishing a Trinitarian terminology also preoccupied certain councils. For instance, the Council of Alexandria of 362 came to the conclusion that, though Eastern and Western texts were using a different terminology to express the mystery of the Trinity, nevertheless their faith was identical. For the teaching of the East, that in God there is one essence — *ousia* — and three *hypostaseis* is identical with that of the West, that God is one *hypostasis* in three Persons. Basil of Caesarea points out the distinction between *ousia* and *hypostasis*, demonstrating that the first term applies to the unity of being, while the second applies to the Trinity of the Persons: '*Ousia*' he writes to Gregory of Nyssa, 'is the ground of the nature common to several [entities] (as for example man, unity, mankind) [applying to] all individuals of our species. *Hypostasis* is the subsistent individual, Peter or Paul'. Applying these distinctions to the Nicene dogma, he indicates that God is one according to nature, essence, but he is Trinitarian according to *hypostasis* (*Epistle* 38; *PG* 32, 325-340).

The issues raised by Nestorius, Eutyches and others brought about a fusion of the dogmatic and liturgical meanings of Trinitarian terminology, so that the same doctrine might be confessed in the same theological terms. A rich philosophical terminology, which in order to express simple nuances altered the terms, brought them together or fused them, is recovered in the difficult process of synodical definition of the revealed truth. According to Gregory of Nazianzus, the alteration of a word or even of a syllable challenged the very existence of the empires. Doctrinal progress was thus made parallel to liturgical and canonical progress.

It is true that any falsification of God's essence cuts man adrift from the source of his existence and from its meaning. His condition, consequently, becomes one of alienation. He is an orphan, estranged from God and cut off both from his fellow-men and from himself, because of the disruptive effect of sin at the very centre of his being. It is important to know what is meant when we speak of God. The powerlessness of theology today is in large part due to the fact that it has reduced God. It has presented a God who is too small, weak, withdrawn. And it is not accidental that reference is often made to the humiliated Servant of Deutero-Isaiah, rather than to the victorious Risen Christ. Erroneous views have reduced him to mere human proportions. Yet the infinite God cannot be diminished. God, by definition, is the Supreme, the Infinite, the Eternal Being who as Creator exercises absolute sovereignty over the whole creation. If we speak of God in lesser terms, we cease to speak of *God* and are speaking instead of a figment of man's imagination or a projection of his arrogance. We must, as Luther put it, let God be God!

To confine God within any dimension of relativity or contingency is to dethrone him and to bring all things under the chaotic uncertainty of uncontrolled chance, or the ancient Greek εἱμαρμένη. A God who is not completely sovereign is a contradiction in terms. Created reality is the expression of the divine Will, and in its cosmic perfection it reflects the perfect order of the divine Mind. Moreover, as nothing that God does is futile or without purpose, so creation, designed in accordance with the Will of God, is conformed to the purpose of its Creator. All things are from him and through him and to him (Rom. 11:36). That the divine purpose in creation should meet with frustration is unthinkable, for then it could not be the divine purpose. It is unimaginable, likewise, that God should abandon his creation and allow it to collapse into perdition, for this would mean the abandonment and the defeat of his purpose, which in turn would mean that he does not possess that sovereignty which properly belongs to God alone, and therefore that he is not God after all. Such is the dynamic of God's creation and providence.

For the Cappadocians, salvation resulting from Christ constitutes an innovation for fallen human nature, which has not at all altered the *Logos*. The permanent desire of the Creator is that human nature, in its deep ontological nature, despite redemptive action, should remain the same. What must change is the *tropos*, how it exists and how it behaves in our daily dealings. This *tropos hyparxeos* in Adam's humanity was dominated by the attraction of egoistic pleasure, and hence an individualisation, which fragments humanity and delivers it over to corruption. On the contrary, in Christ Incarnate — fruit not of *philautia* through γένεσις but of *philanthropia* through γέννησις — the same nature is established by the Person of Christ who made it his own, in the communion of love and in his divine liberty as Son, assuming the appearance of a slave in order to restore this likeness with the Father (Phil. 2:7). This was realised by the acceptance even of death as the ultimate consequence of sin, by Christ who alone was without sin but incorporated in flesh the pure love of God (Maximus, *Ambigua* 42; *PG* 91, 1341). Therefore the Person of the Son, in assuming our humanity communicates to it his own personal ὑποτύπωσις (*Opuscula theologica et polemica* 20; *PG* 91, 241). Later, in the Church, through Baptism, a sacramental life offers the opportunity to acquire this *hypostasis*, being reborn through the Church, recreated by the Spirit and taking a divine name, belonging to Christ and receiving his name (*Mystagogia* 24; *PG* 91, 712). As Macarius the Egyptian says: 'On account of God's infinite mercy he changes himself, enters into pious souls to be seen and share with them his blessing' — 'μεταβάλλει καὶ σμικρύνει καὶ ἐξομοιεῖ ἑαυτὸν σωματοποιῶν κατὰ χώρησιν' (*Spiritual Homilies* 4, 1).

If such an emphasis was put by the Cappadocians and later by Gregory Palamas on *ousia* and the non-created energies, it was to show God's complete independence: God does not depend on anything, but all things depend on him. Without origin or ἀρχή he possesses existence in himself. This is the meaning of *ousia*, which is derived etymologically from ὁ ὤν, ἡ οὖσα, τὸ ὄν. Thus, *ousia* means the Being par excellence. Furthermore, being beyond human condition, God does not require any external relation or contact — σχέσις. Now, though on account of his essence he is above all relations, by his Will he nevertheless enters into relation with the world which he has created and continuously maintains. This is a paradox. Briefly, in his *ousia* God is immovable, but not immobile. He is in a continuous movement towards his creation for which he shows caring love, being responsible for bringing it to its finality, without bringing about any increase or decrease of his *ousia*.

When, from a human point of view, activity in natural life diminishes, immediately we think of the loss of a certain energy, and, consequently, of a loss of substance. But in God such a reduction is inconceivable because he has never had a beginning and he remains the Lord of all. Equally, it would be unfair to conceive of a God living in self-admiring beatitude, ignoring all happenings around him. Such a God does not exist in Christianity. He is vigilant and continuously intervening in the affairs of the world. The Absolute is not subject to any law other than that of unbounded love — his very Being, in fact. All things are under him and nothing is above him. How can this mystery be explained? Gregory of Nyssa meditates on this point: 'Human spirit reaches the divine, passing by mere phenomena, the more it realises that the divine nature is invisible. In this lies the true knowledge of the object sought, in reaching us and in escaping us' (*De vita Mos.* 2; *PG* 44, 376-377).

Orthodox theology is distinctive in giving priority to ontological reality before nature. Only in such a way is it possible to determine the *tropos* of the essence or of nature. In this sense Gregory Palamas remarks: 'When God answered the question Moses addressed to him he did not say "I am the *ousia*", but "I am the Being". The Being does not come from the essence but on the contrary the essence proceeds from the very Being. He who is the Being includes the existence (*einai*)' (*For the Hesychasts*; ed. Christou, I, 66).

In order to understand the reference of God to any other subject, we have to examine the inner-Trinitarian relationship. God is in continuous contact, not with relative subjects like us, but with the uniquely absolute beings that are his Son and the Spirit. 'If God had been deprived of one of these two, that is, his Son or the Spirit, He could not have been Father', states Symeon the New Theologian (*Hymns*, vol. I, p. 245; ed. Paris 1969). Yet another paradox appears: God condescends to open up relations with created beings, making his absolute being accessible, but without ceasing to maintain his absoluteness. Condescending towards creatures, taking their form, God shows the value he has accorded to this world, but also his plan to confer on them the blessings of a promoted status, that of sonship. This is clearly stated by John of Damascus: 'God the Word has descended from heaven without change; he was manifested on earth, assuming its weakness as a source of elevation' (ὑψοποιὸς κένωσις) (*Encomium II on the Dormition of the Theotokos*). Denys the Areopagite sees a dynamic force for humanity in this *kenosis* (*In divin. nom.*; *PG* 4, 236). Furthermore, the Son's death on Golgotha is not an isolated event in the divine economy, but constitutes a permanent spring of blessing. Thus we have the basis for a continuous communion of men with God. This relationship does not take the form of a cyclic, monotonous repetition, as the ancient philosophers Parmenides and Heraclitus believed, but is inter-personal, God doing everything to make us partakers of his love, i.e. of His life. Where communion is perfect, it is everlasting (John 17: 3).

God's Action in Time and Beyond Space and Time

Time and space, in the context of relation between God and man, have been too much rationalised and absolutised — sometimes with mathematical precision — seen as impenetrable obstacles between the Creator and the creation. We forget that these contingencies are not applicable to God and that the terms used — immutability, activity, movement etc. — are ours, not his. Maximus the Confessor states that the ultimate aim of the descent of the Holy Spirit at Pentecost is permanent union with the creatures, the union of the created with the Logos. Consequently, any other intervention of time as hindrance, and of the natural law of growth, is void. Nothing can prevent God from exercising his prerogatives as the Supreme Ruler of the universe (*Resp. ad Thalassium*; *PG* 90, 760). Human beings are for ever marching towards the infinite, the beyond, the above, the Highest, the unexpected, where time and distance cannot prevail. We feel that all events in the very 'now', the 'present', are relative, phenomenal, temporal, incomplete. We await their perfection and completeness, their change into incorruptibility. We revolt against the emptiness, the nothingness, the meaninglessness of terrestial life compared with the Permanent and Everlasting. Time misused, filled with unworthy deeds or selfish idleness, does not lead to the *real life* but to death. This is for the simple reason, that man in such a situation does not surpass his self; he does not enter therefore into communion with the true 'other', with God, who is the absolute Person, the absolute Source of life, filling and satisfying all.

Basil of Caesarea rightly stated with regard to the subject of *chronos*, time as servant of death, (*Homilies on Hexaemeron* 1, 5; PG 29, 13):

> 'In fact, there did exist something, as it seems, even before the world, to which our minds can attain by contemplation but which has been left uninvestigated because it is not adapted to those who are beginners and as yet infants in understanding. This was a certain condition older than the birth of the world and proper to the supramundane powers, one beyond time, everlasting, without beginning or end. In it the Creator and Producer of all things perfected the works of his art, a spiritual light befitting the blessedness of those who love the Lord, rational and invisible natures, and the whole orderly arrangements of spiritual creatures which surpass our understanding and of which it is impossible even to discover the names. These completely fill the essence of the invisible world, as Paul teaches us when he says "For in him were created all things" whether visible or invisible ... When at length it was necessary for this world also to be added to what already existed, primarily as a place of training and a school for the souls of men, then was created a fit dwelling place for all things in general which are subject to birth and destruction ... In truth, is this not the nature of time, whose past has vanished, whose future is not yet at hand, and whose present escapes perception before it is known?'

Basil here follows Aristotle (*Metaphysics* Δ, 1, 1013a):

> 'Beginning means that part of a thing from which one would start first ... That from which each thing would best be originated ... That from which, *not* as an immanent part, a thing first comes to be, and from which the movement or change naturally first begins ... and so the arts — especially the architectonic arts — are called beginnings.'

The human mind has always been frustrated and em-

barrassed by the creative activity of God from nothing. It is
difficult to understand such a process, for the simple reason that,
surrounded by a material world already created, it is hard to
understand that there was a time when it did not exist. We tend
to believe in an eternal form of matter. Early philosophers gave
different interpretations, assuming that through a long evolution things emerged from a primitive nucleus of matter.
Whatever may be the conclusions of scientists on this theme
which will always occupy the mind, there is complete mystery as
to the real origin of the visible creation. The book of Genesis tells
us in condensed wording that God 'created all things visible and
invisible from nothing'. Theodoretus of Cyr, writing in 429, was
aware of problems such as these, even that of Time as having an
origin, appearing with the Creation. In dealing with adversaries
of the Christian faith, of an intellectual Hellenistic background,
he remarks: 'God needs nothing, while human endeavours need
each other's contribution ... But the Creator of the universe
does not need either instruments or matter. What for other
artists is matter, instrument, labour, time, science and attentive
care, for the God of all is the Will' (*Graecarum affectionum curatio*
114; *PG* 83, 916).

The awareness of χῶρος, 'space', with regard to relationship
indicates a consciousness of the existence of a person, of the
'other'. It does not denote a geometrical distance but a personal
attitude or a personal existence. This is the case with terms used
in the Bible with regard to the sitting of the Son on the right
hand of the Father, eloquently commented on by Athanasius of
Alexandria: 'Sitting on the right does not at all imply that the
Father sits on the left. What is right and honourable for the
Father, that also the Son possesses. He says: "All that my Father
has is mine too" (John 16: 15). Setting the Son on the right
implies that the Father is on the right also. As if he were a human
being, he can say: "I have set the Lord always before me,
because he is at my right hand, I shall not be moved" (Psalm 16:
8)' (*Contra Arianos* 1, 61).

For Basil of Caesarea, time is an interspace inseparable from
the idea of the world, co-extensive with the creation: Χρόνος δὲ
ἐστὶν τὸ συμπαρεκτεινόμενον τῇ συστάσει τοῦ κόσμου διάστημα
(*Adv. Eunom.* 1, 21; *PG* 29, 560). Basil was familiar with the
scientific conceptions of the ancients. Sextus Empiricus (*Adv.*

Math. 3, 107), Chalcidius (*Comment. on Timaeus* 68) and John of Lydia (*De Mens.* 3, 3) had taught an eternal cyclic movement of the universe. Having observed the circular movement of the constellations Aristotle (*Physics 8*, 8, 264), had set out to prove the eternity of the sky. Basil repeats their arguments and images of eternity in order to refute them by proving that the circle starts from a point, therefore inevitably has a first movement and beginning.

Gregory of Nyssa repeats the same argument (*De hominis opificio* 23; *PG* 44, 209), i.e. that movement implies a first cause. Elsewhere, Basil, following Aristotle (*De Coelo* 1, 12, 288b), states that where something is born, inevitably there also exists an anticipated destruction. Aristotle, himself, however, believed in the eternity of the material world: 'That the heaven as a whole neither came into being nor admits of destruction, as some assert, but is one and eternal, with no end or beginning ... we may convince ourselves' (*De Coelo* 2, 1, 283b).

But such ideas of an eternal world lead to pantheism, or identifying it with the Supreme Being, as is attested by Origen: 'The Greeks say plainly that the world as a whole is God; the Stoics, that it is the first God; the followers of Plato, that it is the second; but some of them that it is the third' (*Contra Celsum* 5, 581).

Time and world are two correlated notions. Time begins with the creation of the universe. This universe was not made during time, but along with the creation of time. So time did not pre-exist. What coincides therefore with the creation of the world, is condemned to change and decline, to reduction and final annihilation. Since the world is finite like all creatures, Athanasius of Alexandria remarked:

'It is the property of created things not to exist before their becoming, so that they come out of nothing and have a beginning in their creation; only the *Logos* of God in contrast to creatures which have started to become, has no beginning in his existence and certainly could not begin to exist; because as the Father who has begotten him is eternal, he also is eternal. Created things cannot enjoy eternity, since they have a beginning in existence, they are taken from nothing and did not exist before

becoming. All these which have not existed before they
became, how could they co-exist with God who exists
always? Consequently, those who claim the eternity of
creation are led to the same irrationalism and foolishness
as those who contest the eternity of the Lord of the
creation and Word (*Logos*) of God' (*Contra Arian.* 2, 1, 22;
PG 26, 148, 193, 269 — *Epist. Enc. ad episcopos Aegypti et
Libyae* 8; *PG* 26, 1044).

In the same sense Maximus the Confessor reflected the Patristic
view in saying:

> 'Some claim the eternal co-existence of creatures with
> God, which is quite impossible. For how can being, in all
> points limited, co-exist for eternity with him who is
> absolutely infinite? How can that which is substantially a
> creature be co-eternal with the Creator? That which has
> been produced from nothing cannot in fact become co-
> eternal with that which is without beginning and has
> always existed' (*Centuries on Charity* 4, 6; *PG* 90, 1049).

So far as God's creative energies are concerned, we must
assume that there is no change in his actual nature. God is
Creator eternally and supratemporally, because he has in
himself all that constitutes the Creator, namely the Will to
conceive a plan, to modify it, to carry it out and to provide
aftercare.

An acceptance of evolution moves towards a mechanistic
interpretation of the universe and of mankind. Creation, on the
other hand, demands the introduction of the supernatural; this
is abhorrent to anyone who accepts only scientific data. The
scientists must work out processes. Conversely, the 'creationist'
defends the idea of an eternal God who works in eternity as well
as in time, who is personal and who deals with men personally,
who is therefore not only the 'I am' but also the God of
revelation and communicability with his creation. The word
'evolution' implies that what now appears was latent in the
realm of the potential out of which it evolves. Nothing else is
required; anything more than this leads to confusion.

There will always remain much room for discussion on the
question: How does God who is Spirit relate to matter? Creation

'out of nothing' is a mystery. Creative processes working on matter are also a deep mystery. If God creates, he creates out of nothing. The question becomes very pressing in the relationship between divine sovereignty and human freedom. To say that such areas are shrouded in mystery is in no way to deny their reality. Rather it is to assert that if evidence is derived from a study of the material world according to law and order, then there is no scientific answer to the theological question. In brief, a Christian is forced again and again to have recourse to belief rather than 'evidence'. Epistemologically, we must insist that beginnings for the scientists have to be an assumption, an acceptance in faith.

Working Out our Salvation

The Fathers are often criticised for being defensive and systematically polemical. They appear obsessed with seeing in every opponent a heretic or impostor of the Faith. Thus, the critics say, their writings become monotonous, concerned more with refutation than with construction. This is the case particularly with regard to the whole doctrine of Christology and the Trinity. In fact, the Fathers are both defenders and exponents, apologists and catechists. They seek to refute errors, but at the same time to explain the depth of the Faith.

The term *ousia* might have given the impression that God existed in a kind of impassibility, immutability, indirectly influenced by the ancient Greek philosophical conception of God. Such a view partly influenced even the mediaeval Scholastics, who described God as an immobile, self-centred, eternal substance. Actually, the opposite was the case with the Patristic Fathers: they tried to modify such conceptions whilst keeping intact ancient terms as best expressing Christian truths. Without falling into the other extreme of Hegelian 'becoming', they put forward a living and intervening God as the only answer.

What the hymnographers heard, their pens brought down to earth, enabling the Church to sing in harmony with the angelic choirs. This was the *leitourgia* (lit. function) of the hymnographer, i.e. to unite earth to heaven in one melodious cosmic hymn of praise to the Creator. No *troparion* contains a single static line. Everywhere there is light, movement and music.

Heaven and earth sing together, past and present merge. Eden and Bethlehem become one. The universe is one. All the hymns reveal the eternal and dynamic encounter between God and humanity. We are shown the wholly human response to that mystery which has come upon us, which is beyond ourselves, and yet towards which we strain.

Most of the Orthodox hymns point out the inner consciousness of love, the indwelling of the Spirit, the soul's despair and experimental knowledge of the Trinity. Listen to Symeon the New Theologian (*Hymn* 51): 'And when you envelop me completely, I am filled with sweetness, filled with joyfulness'. Or elsewhere: 'What is important for me really is that which makes me a participant of your unspeakable glory' (*Hymn* 35).

The Ecclesiological Dimension

More emphasis should be placed on the infusion of grace in the Church. Our inquiry will remain incomplete if God's energies are not related to the body of Christ as their channel par excellence. Proceeding from a personal God, they nevertheless aim at building up the society of the redeemed people, the *Laos tou Theou*. It is in the Church that such energies are located and manifested. They have an ecclesial character. They do not operate in disorder or independently. When Pseudo-Denys treats of God's activities, he mentions the divinely established hierarchy, both celestial and ecclesiastical, composed of monks, *celebrants*, *devotees*, *catechumens*, *energumens* and penitents. Since the incarnation of Christ there is a solid ministerial and sacramental structure (*Eccl. Hier.* 5, 7; *PG* 3, 513). He goes on to describe the place of the Eucharist which makes the synaxis (the worshipping assembly) a partaker of God's grace and communion.

However, certain texts of the ascetic Fathers may seem to be mystical, for it is God's sacraments that articulate the life-giving energies for the believers. Gregory Palamas states that entry into membership coincides with man's participation in Christ's renewal of man through Baptism. Thus man is liberated from the burden of sin. Referring to John Chrysostom's text (*Comment. in Johan. Hom.* 85, 3; *PG* 59, 463), he stresses the effect of the Eucharist as conferring the sanctifying action of the Spirit. Hence a new divine life springs up, enabling us to become concorporate with Christ and subsequently shining with divine light (*Ad Xenen monacham*; *PG* 150, 1056). It is clear that for the Fathers the Deity sends out non-participatory (ἀμέθεκτοι) powers, substantial (ὑπερούσιος) or even self- or supra-substantial (αὐθυπερούσιοι, ὑπερούσιοι), but also others which can be shared. Gregory Palamas makes a clear distinction between divine *ousia*, and the divine *dynameis* in which man is invited to participate. But the *ousia* remains incommunicable and undivided, because it is beyond and above name: 'ἀνώνυμον εἶναι, ὡς ὑπερώνυμον καὶ ἀπερινόητον παντελῶς' (Ch. 29). This God beyond *ousia* (ὑπερούσιος) transmits powers (οὐσιώδης), but the component of all this remains 'supra-self-essential' being (ὑπερουσίως ὑπερούσιον) (*Discursus secundus contra secundos*; ed. Christou I, p. 667).

It can be seen that there is an interplay between the μεθεκτός— ἀμέθεκτος of God. God is ἀμέθεκτος as ὑπερούσιος, but μεθεκτός as having power and essential energy (οὐσιοποιός) (*Kephalaia physica* 108). All that surrounds God is not his *ousia*, whereas he remains the *ousia* of all surrounding him (ibid. 3, 2, 25). No single thing of all that is created has, or ever will have, even the slightest communion or contact with the supreme nature (*PG* 150, 1176). These energies are not something that exists apart from God, not a gift which God confers upon man: they are God himself in his action and revelation to the world; God remains complete in each of his divine energies. The world is charged with the grandeur of God; all creation is a gigantic Burning Bush, permeated but not consumed by the ineffable and wondrous fire of God's energies. When we say that the sacraments bestow grace, what we mean is that we have a direct experience of God himself. We know God, that is to say, God in his energies, not in his essence.

The Fathers preserved God's transcendence and avoided the absorption of the human into the divine as a kind of pantheism. Yet they allowed God's immanence, his continuous presence in the world. God remains the other partner, the 'wholly Other'. A sacrament is not the partaking of *something* divine, but of the *Person* who is *Christ*. God is living, acting, continuing his theophany in the Church. The Church is, as it were, *Christus prolongatus*. On this is based the corporateness of ecclesiology. Thus Saint Augustine relates redemption to the immutability of

God: 'Because God is immutable and has made all things out of his mercy, similarly the Son of God has condescended to assume corruptible flesh, remaining all the while the Word (*Verbum*) of God; he has condescended to come down for the benefit of humanity' (*Sermo* 6, 5).

Many of the Fathers take the transcendent action of the Holy Spirit in time and space as eloquent proof of God's continuing involvement, strengthening and sustaining human beings in their spiritual struggle. The culminating point of this action is at Pentecost; during this major Christian feast, truly 'the earth becomes heaven'. The gift of the Spirit at Pentecost made Christ powerfully present in the lives of his disciples, and they began to preach and bear witness to Jesus as the risen Christ, the King and the Lord. For this very reason Pentecost is traditionally called the birthday of the Church. John Chrysostom (347-407) describes the importance of this action of the Holy Trinity in the life of Christians:

> 'This day the earth has become heaven for us. Not because the stars have descended from the heavens to earth, but because the apostles have ascended to heaven by the grace of the Holy Spirit, now abundantly poured forth. So the whole world has been transformed into heaven; not because human nature has been changed, but because there was a change in the direction of the will. For there was found a tax-gatherer, and he was transformed into an evangelist. There was found a persecutor, and he was changed into an apostle. There was found a robber, and he was led into paradise. There was found a prostitute, and she was made the equal of virgins. There were found wise men, and they were taught the Gospels. Evil fled away, and gentleness took its place. Slavery was put away, and freedom came in its stead. All debts were forgiven, and the grace of God was conferred. Therefore earth became heaven: and from repeating this again and again I shall not cease' (*Sermo* 1, *in Pentecosten*; *PG* 52, 803).

More attention should be given to the experience of Christians during liturgical worship. The texts composed reflect exactly this living experience in which God transcends space and time and is with us. Incarnation aims at actualising Christ's presence whenever and wherever the faithful are gathered together in his name. God's Spirit is sent in order to sanctify us and to facilitate our communion with the Trinity. Thus the verbs used by the hymnographers are not in the past, the aorist tense, but the continuous present, in conjunction with such expressions as 'now', 'behold', 'this very moment', 'today'. Time is abolished for God's action, because time belongs to him and he can any moment he wants supersede it for communication with us. During the Eucharist he is asked to send down his Spirit, not because God is somewhere, namely above the earth, or located somewhere requiring him to descend. Such expressions have to be used by us human beings, since we are living here on earth, conditioned by time and space. Orthodox liturgical texts are obliged to actualise in time and space the infinite and the unseen. The commands to 'Eat, drink the very body and blood of Christ', reflect the reality of how Christ, in a miraculous way, is sacrificed and distributed to all the communicants. The great prayer of the blessing of water at Epiphany, attributed to Sophronius, Patriarch of Jerusalem, tries to overcome the inherent materialistic difficulties in the words of invocation: 'O Trinity, beyond all being, supra-essential, more than divine, supremely divine, since you are more than divinity . . .' — 'Τριὰς ὑπερούσιε, ὑπεράγαθε, ὑπέρθεε . . .'. All relevant expressions: visitation of the Spirit, ἐπιφοίτησις, ἐπίκλησις, κατάπεμψις, παρουσία etc., manifest the invisible action of God who is beyond time and space.

As the Fathers understood from the very beginning, the Church is not just a window through which one catches a glimpse of heaven and the metaphysical world. Rather it is the mystical ladder on which man ascends and God descends, so that a real ascent and descent (ἀνάβασις καὶ κατάβασις) take place, resulting in the blessed meeting of Creator and creature. Such an operation has a wholly salutary effect upon man's life, ontologically and eschatologically.

Photius, Patriarch of Constantinople (810-895), left us a wonderful analogy when he compared the task of the Church to that of a vehicle or ferryboat which comes to mankind from the celestial coast, conveying to all of us the divine compassion, the overwhelming grace of God's philanthropy: 'διαπορθμεύει ἡμῖν τὴν ἐκεῖθεν ἀγαθοειδῆ καὶ θείαν εὐμένειαν' (*Amphilochia: Quaestiones* III; *PG* 101, 656).

Our God is, in other words, a committed God, involved in the restoration of mankind. He is infinitely near to us. He is at the very heart of our history. Our God is a passionate God. But this relationship between God and humanity is worked out through his people; it has both a divine and a social dimension. It is a cause of unity and brotherhood, as Saint Augustine recalls when speaking of the Eucharist: 'The virtue that this bread contains is unity, and made into his body and changed into his limbs, we must begin to be what we receive' (*Sermo* 57, 7, 7; PL 38, 389).

More study is needed of the contemporaneity produced by this communion of the assembly with the Holy Trinity, especially when in the West there is hesitation in assigning a creative or cosmic role to the Spirit (cf. C. D. Moule: *The Holy Spirit*, Oxford, 1978). There is even doubt as to whether 'invocation' is ever realistic, on the ground that, since the Spirit is immanent within us, we cannot 'call him down' in our worship. Certainly, the Spirit is within us and everywhere, filling the whole universe. But for solemn manifestations of the people of God, a special infusion of it must be sought, since it concerns not an isolated individual, but the whole Body of Christ. The phrase 'calling down', involving descent or ascent or any other term taken from human vocabulary, proves our limitations in describing the unseen realities. Indeed, most of the terms found in liturgical prayers involve metaphor which should not be taken literally.

Conclusion

To a certain extent the dissatisfaction expressed at the use by the early Fathers of Aristotelian terms, and notably the desire to make less use of terms such as 'essence' and 'energies', is very understandable. Whatever arguments may be advanced in their favour, they still risk being misunderstood on account of their impersonal character. It might be better to use more intimate and personal expressions, such as 'communion with the Holy Spirit', more in line with those of the OT and more connected with the historical Jesus. All modern anxiety about the absence of personal communion in human life and with God, could thus be overcome, reassuring man in his loneliness and anguish that he can be visited and sustained, not by vague, immaterial, heavenly forces, but above all by God's personal intervention. A God who is reluctant to be with us, who sends us alternative powers and energies, contradicts the very sense of Christ's Incarnation. Let us not forget that at the very beginning of the Orthodox Liturgy, we praise the Holy Trinity, God's Kingdom, Triune, and we are thus given the assurance that the Three Persons are present as concelebrants; we ourselves are solemnly dedicated to them through Eucharistic worship. We therefore expect a live, interpersonal communion, epicletic and doxological.

It follows that no system of theological terminology or investigation can be absolutised. Gregory Palamas, long ago (1296-1359), saw cataphatism and apophatism as mutually complementary and interrelated. There are even cases where *cataphasis* may have the force of *apophasis* (*Natural Chapters* 123). This Archbishop of Thessalonica was less interested in wording and formulations than in spiritual realities. Words are not absolutes. They can be changed in order better to serve the articulation of divine truths, as he confesses (see the *Synodical Tome* of 1351, drawn up during the reign of John Cantacuzene against Barlaam and Acindynus). If the economic mystery of the Trinity cannot be entirely explained, at least certain glimpses of it should be made intelligible. Already knowledge of the incomprehensibility of the divine nature is a step forward, and is in itself an experience of the divine.

It is equally true that, by overstressing one aspect with regard to another, certain doctors often appear unable to keep a proper balance. This is the case of Pseudo-Denys. Of course, God in his *Corpus Areopagiticum* is at a distance from the God of neoplatonism; he is not identical with the world or with beings, nor is his *ekstasis* similar to that of Plotinus' God, which is an effusion into which man is absorbed by the unique One. Contrary to Plotinus, who rejects any form of communion with the divine, Denys defends the notion of communion, though admitting that its mode is unknown. The analogy of a circle sending out rays is not very sound, for the simple reason that it departs from the doctrine of *personal* hypostatic union so dear to the Cappadocians.

Admittedly, certain expressions borrowed from philosophy

can irritate modern readers. We know that the Neoplatonic writers of the 5th century taught that creation was the product of the One, single, transcendent Being. But for them the creation was due to necessity — the outpouring of an excessively abundant essence of God, the force of propulsion determining the degree of distance from the One single Being. The nearer a being is to the One, which Plotinus calls νοῦς, the more perfect it is. Intermediate stages serve as links between the superior and the inferior for achieving progress towards the One, through descent and ascent — κατάβασις and ἀνάβασις — a favourite teaching of the Neoplatonist Proclus, and also of Gregory of Nyssa. In descending to the world, the divine energies suffer a kind of veiling. Only those beings close to the upper sphere of the divine can feel God's presence. Exaggerated mysticism could lead to the conclusion that God is so far removed from humanity that desperate efforts are required to obtain his intervention. We are then far from the OT promise to make us God's people, the New Israel, the redeemed heirs of his Kingdom, endowed with Pauline παρρησία, brothers of one another by grace and bearers of the Spirit (πνευματοφόροι), incorporated into Christ's Body and enjoying all the spiritual gifts that membership of the Church provides.

These are but some of the inconveniences of an impersonal view of the divine energies.

* * *

Nobody would disagree with the clear summary so well formulated by Professor Torrance distinguishing determinism and creation, especially during the Nicene period, emphasising the Incarnation of the *Logos* in the spatial and temporal structures of created reality. Far from being immanently bound up with the universe, God remains eternally and transcendentally free, the *Pantocrator* over all space and time. The whole cosmos is not an emanation from the essence of God. It came into existence out of nothing, freely by the Will, Power and, above all, the Love of God, as utterly distinct from God. In creating this universe out of nothing, God has conferred upon it a contingent rationality, as distinct from his own, as creaturely being is from his divine Being. Such views have influenced scientists considerably, turning them away from any dualistic cosmology or epistemology. The impassibility and immutability of God cannot be identified with the Aristotelian notion of the Unmoved Mover, for the simple reason that the Christian God is Person; he loves, wills and acts; therefore he is not centred on eternal stability and blessedness. He is an 'autokinetic' God, who out of his fullness is a *Koinōnia* of Love, through self-emptying (κένωσις). Such an approach helps one to understand the interlocking of God's Reality with worldly reality.

Over against the static conceptions prevailing in Platonic, Aristotelian, Stoic and Neoplatonic circles, the Fathers developed a theology and Christology that were *active*, postulating a Creator ready to help and to descend, since he cannot carelessly abandon that which he has created in his wisdom, and which is, moreover, qualified as being 'very good' (λίαν καλόν). The creation moves within set prescriptions, established and controlled by the *Kyrios* of the visible and invisible world.

God is known through all and even without all; through knowledge but also through *agnosia*. In him are inherent all the faculties in their most perfect state: word, science, contact, feeling, glory, imagination and name and all the rest . . . Yet God is neither understood, nor spoken of, nor named. There is nowhere among beings, nor in any of the beings, anything with which he can be identified. He is praised by all beings everywhere according to the analogy of all, of which he is the very Cause (Maximus the Confessor, *In div. nom.* 7).

In conclusion, as Maximus the Confessor says: 'We have to understand God as having no relations with other beings. The unique Cause of beings is above the beings. Hence God is examined theologically everywhere and nowhere. Since he is found nowhere, all are in him and through him, all being nothing in relation to him. He is found in no place and yet fills all, since he is present everywhere . . .' (*PG* 4, 204).

Since Orthodox worship reflects the faith of the Church, the congregation sings what it believes. The consciousness of the continuous presence and transcendence of the Trinity over time and space, reaching into the daily life of this world without altering God himself, is sung at many moments of the liturgical year, and especially during the feast of the Presentation of our Lord (τῆς Ὑπαπαντῆς): in a hymn attributed to John the Monk:

'He who is without beginning
the *Logos* of the Father,
has made a beginning in time,
without forsaking his divinity'.

Ὁ Ἄναρχος Λόγος τοῦ Πατρὸς
ἀρχὴν λαβὼν χρονικήν,
μὴ ἐκστὰς τῆς αὐτοῦ θεότητος᾽ (*Vespers*, Tone 6).

CHAPTER 3

THE AUTHORITY OF THE CHURCH AND AUTHORITY IN THE CHURCH ACCORDING TO THE REFORMED TRADITION

HANS-HELMUT ESSER

The sole authority over and in the Reformed Church is Jesus Christ himself, the Lord of the Church.[1] All human action in the Church is at the *service* of this authority.[2] This authority becomes a reality in our midst with the sending of the Holy Spirit through the medium of the preached Word which appeals always to the authority of the written Word in Holy Scripture.[3] The sacraments confirm and seal the authority of Jesus Christ promised in the Word of God.

With this basic thesis, the Reformed doctrine of the authority of the Church marks itself off from both a hierarchical and a democratic view of church authority and utterly opposes all anarchy and arbitrariness in the Church. It understands ecclesiology as derivative from Christology.[4] Even in ecclesiology, therefore, it seeks to do justice to the Chalcedonian formula; in other words, in the interests of the authority of Christ himself, to clear the area which lies between the monophysite error on the one side and the dyophysite error on the other. In other words, no triumphalist identification of the Church's authority with the Divinity of Christ, but also no sceptical *a priori* divorce between the lowliness of the Church and the promise of the presence of its Risen Lord! This aversion to any identification in either of these directions reinforces an 'open Christology' over against an autonomous ecclesiology. The Church is understood in a dynamic sense as *creatura Verbi* which continues to depend in hope on the ever renewed grace of the Triune God towards it: *ecclesia reformata semper reformanda Verbo Dei*.[5]

The question put to the Reformed Church by the Orthodox

Church as a Church with a strict hierarchical and episcopal order takes two forms: firstly; how can there be any authority and oversight (*episkopē*) at all in a non-episcopally ordered Church? and secondly; what authority does the World Alliance of Reformed Churches have vis-à-vis its member churches to secure their binding acceptance of ecumenical consensus statements?

There is one comprehensive answer: from its very origins in the Reformation period, the Reformed Church has taught and practiced the *disciplina* as a third *nota ecclesiae* in church life, alongside the pure proclamation of God's Word and the administration of the sacraments in accordance with Holy Scripture. *Disciplina* is taken to mean a disciplined paracletic and paraenetic conduct *subject to* the Gospel, to which congregations and churches are committed. Reformed confessional documents are either an integral part of church order or else closely connected to such order in a temporal way.[6] Being thus closely connected with the *disciplina*, church authority is understood primarily in dynamic and functional rather than in personal and monarchical terms.[7] The *disciplina* derives its claim to acceptance from the all-inclusive reality of the living Word of God and not primarily from legal provisions or from the appellate authority of church courts (presbyteries, synods, disciplinary commissions) whose business is to safeguard discipline. It is assumed here, of course, that these courts are constituted in accordance with church order.

The above comprehensive answer presupposes agreement, of course, that there must be a secondary derived authority in the Church. Agreement in the details of the actual use of such authority and on the theological basis for its exercise will be forthcoming to the extent that such authority must be historically grounded in the special canonical time of Jesus Christ and his apostles. The problem lies in the broad or narrow view taken of the *apostolic tradition*, and in the predominantly horizontal or predominantly vertical interpretation of the *apostolic succession*. Another convergence of views emerges when we define church 'authority' as *historical*, as a present *force of weight and power* (cf. Heb. *kabod*), proceeding from the Triune God (see above) and at the same time at work authoritatively and mysteriously in the continuity of ministerial church action and never without a tradition in this continuity. This comprehensive definition takes seriously the historical priority (*prius*) of God, which has preceded and precedes all human action.

The Reformed Church with its Reformation 'Scripture principle' — the *sola scriptura* — is conscious of standing within this apostolic tradition. It considers this canonicity of Scripture sufficient and it measures later church tradition, including the continued production of confessions of faith, by whether or not it is grounded in the Scriptures and necessarily gives expression to the tendencies of Holy Scripture. The Reformed Church is conscious of standing in the apostolic succession to the extent that, in its contemporary proclamation, it continues the apostolic witness of the New Testament, inseparably connected with the Old Testament in the one salvation-history, and accepts responsibility for the continuation of this proclamation into the future. It respects the succession transmitted within the horizontal dimension of history by the imposition of hands, but does not consider it as indispensable for the being of the Church or as a sign of the superior earthly authority of one church over against another church.[8] The ordination of Reformed pastors with the imposition of hands in accordance with church order serves the vertical dimension of apostolic succession, the *verbi divini ministerium*.[9]

The New Testament presents three arrangements of orderly church leadership: the collegial charismatic order, without a fixed structure of ministries (cf. the Johannine letters); the presbyteral structure of church leadership (cf. 1 Cor. 12; Rom. 12; Letter to the Philippians); and the episcopal order (Pastoral Letters, esp. 1 Tim.).[10]

In the Reformation period, especially where the church had to be completely rebuilt, the Reformed Church decided in favour of the *early Pauline* form of order, not just because of its historically conditioned alienation from the hierarchically ordered Church, and yet not because of its commitment to it as an exclusive principle either. Out of the local form of the presbyterially structured congregational leadership the presbyterial, synodal order was developed for the regional, national and supranational ecumenical levels.[11] In the four hundred years of its history this church order has helped to promote the maturity and self-reliance of congregations. It seems to have had two advantages: the cooperation of theologians and laity in the ministries of the preacher, the teacher, the elder, the deacon; it takes into account on the one hand, the equipment of *many* church members for ministry, and on the other hand, it represents in the simplest orderly way the *grouping* of ministry-enabling services in the four offices of leadership. (Historically it is worth remembering that under the influence of Calvin and Beza a representative principle of delegation prevailed at all levels of this church order in opposition to a direct democratic system such as was proposed by Petrus Ramus and Morelli in the history of the French Reformation.)

In the view of the Reformation, the official ministries, in the exercise of their ministerial authority, do not stand over against the congregation in a fixed customary status but only as they carry out their functions at any given time.[12] In each of these offices, the person exercising ministry knows him or herself to be the first to be addressed by the divine message, the offer of God's grace and the divine exhortation. The We-form is preferred in the preaching of the Gospel. The view of the ministry thus described brings out the fact that the Church's authority does not depend on the perfect *opus operatum* of the officeholder but on the free grace of God in sermon, sacraments and sanctification. The authority to forgive sins is likewise exercised both in the pronouncement of the Gospel following the declaration of 'public guilt' in the assembled congregation, and in the personal pastoral declaration of the pastor or elder (office of the keys).[13] This emphasis on the source of their ministerial functions in Word and Spirit is designed to render those performing the ministry impervious to pressures from political groups whether in social matters or church affairs.[14]

The synodal order of the doctrinal authority of the Church as practised *within* the Reformed Church has immediate implications for the authority of *ecumenical* consensus statements, including those which are conciliar in character. (One striking illustration of the reliability of such binding consensus agreements for the Reformed churches is provided by their treatment of the Leuenberg Agreement.)

The wide influence of synodal decisions is guaranteed in principle by the equal representation of theologians and non-theologians in the composition of Reformed synods at all levels. The non-theologians in particular assume a particularly active responsibility for the acceptance and implementation of decisions in whose drafting they have themselves played a creative part. In virtue of its wide lateral influence the presbyteral-synodal principle has also established itself in many Lutheran churches in central Europe since the nineteenth century.[15] The Reformed Church has developed the following criteria for all synodal declarations:

(a) The need to articulate intelligibly and unambiguously the arguments for those decisions, which are important for the orientation of doctrine and life in terms of Holy Scripture, continuity with the confession of past generations and in fidelity to the call of the Triune God in the contemporary situation.

(b) The need for maximum unanimity in the formulation of such important synodal decisions (homothumadon — Rom. 15: 6 and frequently).

(c) When decisions are not unanimous in questions of doctrine and life, the need to publicise the voting figures and the view of the minority.

These criteria make it easier for church members to make a spiritual appraisal of synodal decisions arrived at in a spiritual manner.[16]

Since all issues are dealt with cumulatively *within* the church from the congregations up to the next higher responsible court, all decisions taken at the level of the World Alliance and all consensus statements resulting from ecumenical dialogues are examined in a spiritual way similarly 'from below upwards' by presbyteries and synods and, when they are confirmed and accepted in these courts, acquire a basis of trust and authority which is generally binding for the whole Reformed Church.

By the practice of actual authority while maintaining the freedom of the Authority of Jesus Christ, this process acts as a bar to any merely legalistic implementation of doctrinal decisions via hierarchical channels, and therefore to the paralysing legalising of dogma from which the Roman Catholic Church, for example, has found it so difficult to extricate itself and which imposes on the laity merely a *fides implicita* thereby weakening its ability to account for its faith and so to bear its witness in the secular world. The spiritual authority we have described as attempted and practised in the Reformed Church encourages obedience to the injunction to 'account for the faith that is within you to anyone who asks you the reason for it' (1 Pet. 3: 15), i.e. the capacity of each member of the Church to have a *fides explicita*, the priesthood of all believers (1 Pet. 2: 9).

The Reformed way of achieving authority, with its stress on spiritual *substance* on a broad basis and its structural involvement of many people is not opposed in an *exclusive way* to an authority with its focus in individual hierarchical persons, nor is it intended to replace such an hierarchical pattern with a representative structure of decision making. A *mutual recognition* of both forms of church order, without any out-of-place feelings of superiority on the one side or the other, would constitute an important step in the direction of closer spiritual unity in the ecumenical movement. This mutual recognition will be achieved by taking seriously the 'open Authority' of Jesus Christ in which both partners heed together the insights into Holy Scripture vouchsafed to us *today* and start afresh from the common basic dogmas of early Christianity. The Reformed view that the authority of the confessional documents is not complete and that these confessions are only *norma normata* subject to the *norma normans* of Holy Scripture is favourable to agreement.

The way in which authority is conceived and practised in the service of the *one* authority of Jesus Christ, and these various forms are always dependent on historical developments, counts among the different gifts, ministries and capacities which have their source and their goal in the one Spirit, the *one* Lord, the *one* God 'who inspires them all in every one' (1 Cor. 12: 5 & 6).

* * *

NOTES

1. Cf. Phil. 2: 9-11; Mt. 28: 18-20 etc. etc.
2. Cf. Mt. 23: 8-12; Mt. 20: 25-28.
3. *The Barmen Declaration* (*May, 1934*): Thesis 1. 'Jesus Christ, as he is testified to us in Holy Scripture is the One Word of God, which we have to hear and which we have to trust and obey in life and in death' (Wilhelm Niesel, *Reformed Symbolics*, tr. D. Lewis, Oliver & Boyd, 1962, p. 358).
    Idem. Thesis 3: 'The Christian Church is the community of brethren

in which Jesus Christ acts presently as Lord in Word and Sacrament by the Holy Spirit. As the Church of pardoned sinners, in the midst of a sinful world it has to witness by its faith and obedience, its message and its order, that it is his alone, that it lives and desires to live only by his consolation and by his orders, in expectation of his coming' (Niesel, *op. cit.* p. 359).

Idem. Thesis 4: 'The various ministries in the Church do not provide for any lordship of some over others, but only for the exercise of that service which is entrusted to and required of the whole congregation' (*ibid.* p. 359).

Emden Synod 1571, Art. 1: 'No congregation (Church) may arrogate to itself the primacy or sovereignty over the other congregations, no preacher claim such primacy or sovereignty over other preachers, no elder over other elders, no deacon over other deacons. Each must even guard most carefully against all suspicion of such arrogance and against every attempt to claim to rule' (original German in P. Jacobs, ed., *Reformierte Bekenntnisschriften und Kirchenordnungen*, Neukirchen 1949, p. 252).

Second Helvetic Confession of 1566, Art. 18: 'The Lord reserves the true authority to himself . . . and remits it to no other so as himself to stand idly by as the mere onlooker watching his busy servants' (original German in Jacobs, *op. cit.* p. 223).

4. *Heidelberg Catechism (1563)* Question 54: 'What do you believe concerning the Holy Catholic Church? That . . . the Son of God, by his Spirit and Word, gathers, protects and preserves for himself . . . a congregation chosen for eternal life . . .' (400th Anniversary Edition, United Church Press, Philadelphia, Boston, 1962, 1963).

5. *Second Helvetic Confession 1566*, Art. 1: 'The preaching of the Word of God is God's Word. When this Word of God is preached in the Church today by duly called preachers, therefore, we believe that God's Word itself is proclaimed and received by the faithful and that we may not devise or expect from heaven any other Word of God; likewise we must in every case attend to the Word itself which is proclaimed and not to the servant who proclaims it' (German text in Jacobs, *op. cit.* p. 178).

6. Cf. the relation between the Geneva Catechism and the Geneva Church Order 1541-42 and 1541-1561 (see notes in Niesel, ed. *Bekenntnisschriften und Kirchenordnungen Der Nach Gottes Wort Reformierten Kirche*, 3rd ed. Zürich 1938, p. 1ff and p. 42); the relation between *Confession de Foy* and *Discipline Ecclésiastique*, both of 1559 (see Niesel, *op. cit. Bekenntnisschriften etc.* p. 65ff.); also the Heidelberg Catechism as part of the Palatinate Church Order of 1563 (Niesel, *op. cit.* p. 136ff.).

7. Cf. Mt. 18, cited in the doctrine of the office of the keys in the Heidelberg Catechism, QQ 83-85.

8. Cf. *Netherlands Confession (1561)*, Art. 29: 'So far as the false Church is concerned, it attaches far more importance to itself and its institutions than to God's Word . . . It relies more on human beings than on Jesus Christ . . .' (original in Jacobs, *op. cit.* p. 168).

The Confessio Scotica (1561), Art. 18: 'The nottis, signes, and assurit tokenis, quhairby the Immaculate spouse of Christ Jesus is knawin from that horrible harlot, the Kirk malignant, we affirme ar neyther antiquitie, tytle usurpit, lineal descence ...' (Niesel, *op. cit. Bekenntnisschriften etc.* p. 102). Cf. also *Second Helvetic Confession* 17, *op. cit.* p. 212ff.

9. *Second Helvetic Confession (1566)* 18: 'Ordination. And the elected persons should be ordained by the elders with public prayers and the imposition of hands. We here condemn all who put themselves forward on their own initiative even though they have neither been elected nor sent nor ordained ...' (in Jacobs, *op. cit.* p. 221).

   Emden Synod, Art. 16: 'The ministers of the Word are examined by those by whom they are elected' (Consistory with the judgement and endorsement of the classis). 'If their doctrine and life are approved, they are confirmed in their ministry with solemn prayers and the imposition of hands. This latter is for the congregations to decide in freedom and remains untainted by all superstition' (in Jacobs, *op. cit.* p. 253).

10. Cf. H. v. Campenhausen, *Kirchliches Amt und geistliche Vollmacht in den ersten drei Jahrhunderten*, 2nd ed. 1963. H. H. Esser, 'Geistlicher Aufbau und innere Ordnung der Gemeinde' in *Emden 1571-1971, 400 Jahre Emder Synode*, 1973, pp. 167-182.

11. Cf. Emden Synod: On the presbytery meetings, on the provincial synod; on the general synods (in Jacobs, *op. cit.* p. 259ff.).

12. Cf. note 3 above, *Barmen Declaration* 3 and 4. Also 'Theses of the Moderamen of the Reformed Alliance on the Significance of the Reformed Confession for the structure of the Evangelical Church in Germany and its member churches' (German text in EPD *Dokumentation* 1972, pp. 164-170, 3.2).

13. See note 7 above. Also the church orders (in Jacobs *op. cit.*) or *Confession de Foy*, Art. 25 and 29 as examples.

14. See *Reformed Moderamen Theses*, 3.5.

15. An excellent example of the ordering and practice of synodal authority linking all decision-making processes back to the congregational level is provided by the Würzburger Synod of the Roman Catholic German Episcopal Conference, composed of both theologians and laity. Cf. 'Gemeinsame Synode der Bistümer in der Bundesrepublik Deutschland, Beschlusse der Vollversammlung', Freiburg, Basel, Wien, 1976.

16. Cf. *Reformed Moderamen Theses*, Thesis 4 to 4.3.

CHAPTER 4

AUTHORITY IN THE ORTHODOX CHURCH

CHRYSOSTOMOS KONSTANTINIDIS

Christocentrism of the issue

All sense of power and authority within Christianity should be understood, fundamentally and solely, according to the pattern set by the life and practice of Jesus Christ. Teaching on authority in the Church relies entirely on a christocentric model of authority. Authority in the Church cannot be understood except as stemming exclusively and definitively from the Lord.

If we analyse this conception, we find that Jesus, in his earthly life as in his risen and glorified state — according to the clear indications of the New Testament — taught and practised a form of authority linked on the one hand to the principle of his eternal and immutable 'sonship' in relation to the Father within the communion of the Holy Trinity, and, on the other hand, to the principle of his 'brotherhood' in relation to the apostles, that is, the type of bond existing between master and disciples.

It follows that all attempts to define ecclesiastical authority will move between these poles: our Lord's kinship with the Father, on the one hand, and the bond between master and disciples, on the other.

One must, however, exempt his absolute 'authority' over death and the devil. Over these he had complete mastery.

It goes without saying that this christocentric perspective of authority in the New Testament differs from that of the Old Testament. According to the latter, the authority of Yahweh over mankind in general and over his chosen people in particular was absolute. This exclusivity was evident even in the 'alliance' between Yahweh and the children of Israel, for this 'alliance' did but fortify and ratify his existing authority, laying down the norms of future relations between God invested with authority and the Jew set under him. Only through Jesus Christ are these norms abolished and superseded by the entry into a 'new alliance', which is *in Christo*. Jesus Christ gives men the right to turn 'slavery' into 'sonship': 'To all who received him . . . he gave power to become children of God' (John 1:12). In fact, this 'sonship' is a form of 'communion', bringing God to mankind and mankind to God. It is not absolute power, nor a suppression of cordial relations, nor a polarisation between the absolute entity and a relative creation.

This means that, in speaking of authority in the Church, we cannot entertain any notion of absolute power. Nor can there be a polarisation within ecclesiastical authority between a despotic organ or person and a blind, utterly passive subject; nor yet an uncontrolled and independent exercise of power on both sides, without the befitting objective criteria.

From this one may conclude that in the Church the pattern of authority set by our Lord is one of communion and 'non-absoluteness', in accordance with the New Testament image of Christ's example.

New Testament terminology

It should be recalled straightaway that the New Testament use of terms like 'power' (and 'powers'), 'strength' (and 'forces') 'dominion' (and 'dominions') is not the equivalent of 'authority'. Often the two concur. But they refer either to the heavenly powers, to worldly powers or to the Lord himself in the sense that he exercises dominion over all these powers.

It is not uncommon for our Lord to be termed a 'slave'. He is often called a 'sign', especially a sign of contradiction given 'for the fall and rising of many' (Luke 2:34). He is referred to as a 'sign', meaning the manifestation of his divinity, not as an autocratic deity, but as one of service and offering, as manifested in his miracles, his healings, his raising of the dead, his everyday dealings with those round him.

Within this phraseological framework it can easily be seen why the term 'power' is never directly attributed to him. Our Lord is, of course, considered a 'prophet, mighty in deed and word'; but with the corollary that this strong man has been handed over by the chief priests and rulers to be put to death (Luke 24:19).

The term 'authority' is used quite differently. It is clearly applied to the authority which our Lord possessed from his Father and passed on, under certain conditions, to his disciples. It is therefore not wrong to assert that this term is the clue to the whole New Testament terminology on 'authority'.

Although the term 'authority' (*exousia*) is used in all ninety five times in the New Testament, in the Synoptics it applies only seven times to our Lord. Out of the seven, five cases refer to the power he holds from his Father and which he transmitted to the disciples in order to cast out demons, or to forgive sins and heal (Matt. 10:1; Mark 3:15 and 6:7; Luke 9:1 and 10:19).

In John, the 'authority' which the Father gave to the Son and which the latter exercises during his earthly life, refers consecutively to the judgement he is entitled to exercise over the quick and the dead (5:27), to his powers in laying down his life and receiving it back of his own free will (10:18), and, finally, to his being sovereign over all mankind, in order to give it eternal life (17:2). It goes without saying that this authority is an exclusive mark, quality and property of the Son and relates to his threefold attributes as awaited Messiah, Saviour and future Judge.

Without doubt we are faced here with the quintessence of authority, which is, properly speaking, that of the Lord. It is his distinctive hallmark, it fully befits his person, and it is this which he handed on to the apostles and to his Church. The absolutely christocentric dimension of this authority ever since in the Church is quite clear.

On this score, among all the relevant texts in the New Testament one stands out, the famous passage in Matthew 28; for it refers to the moment and the mode of transmission of authority and power from the Lord to the apostles and the Church. It occurs during the post-resurrection period. The recipients are the eleven apostles.

> All authority in heaven and on earth has been given to me. Go forth therefore and make disciples of all nations, baptizing them in the name of the Father and the Son and the Holy Spirit, teaching them to observe all that I have commanded you; and lo, I am with you always, to the close of the age.

God, the Word of God, transmits his own power and authority to the eleven men-apostles. This is a guarantee that henceforth men will be able to participate in God's active authority, exercising it in his name, being invested with it and able to transmit it, integrally, validly and officially, when the time comes to do so. There is a natural proviso that the men who will receive it will prove themselves truly worthy of such an honour and distinction (only the eleven were present and no-one else — who might have been unworthy); and inasmuch as both its immediate receivers and those of following generations could prove themselves blameless and would speak 'in demonstration of the Spirit and power', their faith 'would not rest in the wisdom of men but in the power of God' (1 Col. 2:4-5).

The extension of this institution of transmitting authority by the Lord to the apostles and by them to others, who, on the ecclesiological plane, make up the Church, is described by St. Paul in a well-known passage of 1 Corinthians on the Holy Spirit, where he speaks of the gifts of the Spirit, and of the various ministries which the Spirit has called into being in the Church (1 Cor. 12:4-11).

It now needs to be established what actual types of authority developed in the Early Church.

Authority in the Early Church

Before enumerating the various types of authority in the Church, it is wise to consider some of the basic pneumatological and ecclesiological factors in force at the time.

It should be said at the start that our Lord intended and announced that transmission of power and authority by the apostles to the Church should take place, through his own mediation under the supernatural guidance of the Paraclete. This was to be the role of the Holy Spirit, who has divinely appointed authority to guide the Church in future 'into all truth' (John 16:13). That which is to prevail in the Church and the life of the faithful in general, over the question of ecclesiastical authority, should and does always bear the stamp of the Paraclete ever since. In his name alone will all forms of authority be exercised. The pneumatological factor will always remain the weightiest and most important coefficient for the exercise of ecclesiastical authority.

Alongside this pneumatological element is to be set the faithfulness on the part of man to the doctrine and tradition of truth entrusted thus authoritatively. Accepting *a priori* the authority of the Lord and the Paraclete (as witnessed in the revealed and transmitted doctrine of truth) he will participate in it *de facto* by means of a concrete and clear reception, preservation, confession, transmission and traditional rendering of this truth, projected authoritatively in the faith. It will thereby be assured of an incorruptible extension, 'to the close of the age', in an eschatological perspective.

It is self-evident that the believer, appearing as a factor on the scene of authority, also has the Holy Spirit as the guarantor of authority. Ever since the day of Pentecost, it is the Spirit who sets the seal on every utterance and interpretation of the truth received (Matt. 10:20), and who journeys alongside the faithful, truth-endowed believer (Acts 16:6ff.). Above all, he assists in every act at the nomination of suitable persons to be in charge of the Church, such as have a true vocation from God and the mission to watch diligently over the truth revealed and handed down. This is firmly and forcefully stated in Scripture: 'Take heed to yourselves and to all the flock, in which the Holy Spirit has made you guardians . . .' (Acts 20:28).

So the Church succeeded to the apostles, with its organs of government. Here we speak no longer of the narrow or wider circle of apostles, nor only of the three thousand on the day of Pentecost, or of a similar number of adherents, but of all the apostles together, who comprise 'the company of those that believed' (Acts 4:32), the deacons or servers (Acts 6:2; I Tim. 3:8-13), the presbyters or elders (I Tim. 5:17), and of course, as we have seen, the *episcopoi* or 'overseer-bishops' (I Tim. 3:1-7; Titus 1:5). These were the immediate institutional wielders of apostolic authority amid the 'company of those that believed', the 'charismatics', the figures of authority and service in the Church. At the same time these were to be considered only as guarantors and authoritative members of the *communio* which our Lord instituted and which the Holy Spirit nourishes and assists by the gift of grace.

Thus, according to plan, there came about with the passage of time the well-known reference of all these to their predecessors of yore and through them to the apostles, or to one of the apostles, or at least to one of the heroes and martyrs of the faith, as being closer to the actual person of Jesus Christ. Thus there evolved the well known concept of the 'apostolicity' of the local Churches, and the principle of apostolic succession, which has been in vigour ever since. By reference to it, every Church and charismatic bearer of ecclesiastical authority could claim to be in touch with the unique authority of the Lord Jesus.

Seen from this angle, ecclesiastical authority as it thus came to be recognised is basically a communion in the truth and teaching handed down in the Church, by divine authority, through the Lord and his apostles after him. This church authority is effectively safeguarded only by the absolute faithfulness of the local churches to the catholic spirit of this communion of participation. Conversely, every break in communion, every movement away from this participation, signifies a loss of the visible evidence of authority for those who bring it about.

The spread of 'episcopal' authority

From the aforegoing it has been shown how authority in the Early Church came to be crystallised in a line of succession involving the person of the local church pastor, and in particular the local bishop. So, immediately following the so-called strictly apostolic period, in the West as much as in the East, there gradually arose the ecclesiastical practice of investing one particular leading figure from each worshipping community with pastoral authority extending over all the community. That person was the bishop.

The local bishop's position, multiple pastoral responsibility and obligation to abide by the authority of our Lord and his apostles are outlined already by St. Paul, to a large extent in his apostolic activity and preaching, but more especially in his pastoral letters.

Ignatius of Antioch is the first — at least in the Christian East — to give a broad theological base to the role, place and task of the bishop on the level of authority. He proclaims that obedience to the bishop is tantamount to obedience to God (*Magn.* iii. 1-2; vi. 1; *Trall.* ii. 1). Here the whole theme undergoes a clear development, with the definite entry of the bishop as sole wielder of the power of authority in the Church.

Not as an absolute or autocratic figure, but as one who derives his authority from the theological and ecclesiological principle (the only one valid) which identifies power and authority with God, and God alone. For God is the sole authority. It is his authority which is represented and placed in the bishop. The bishop is merely the visible sign of this authority, the point to which the faithful look in seeking for true authority in the Church.

This important role attributed by Ignatius to the bishop had two other aspects. One was that just as he issued from the midst of the worshipping community, so he was called upon to serve it and to enjoy the moral, usually also the vocal, support of his flock. The other was that he was installed and ordained to his task of authority by the joint sacramental witness of his fellow bishops (in co-ordaining him, if not always in co-nominating him). By these means, the widest possible communion with the Lord's authority, as handed down by the apostles in the Church, was ensured in his person.

As such opportunities grew in the Church, the ground was laid for the emergence of ecclesiastical synods, made up of several bishops belonging to the same region or to a wider circle, in order to deal with the various problems besetting the Church. This was before synods became the objects of theology and canon law. It was a fortunate experience for the Church. It has in its favour the essential mark of apostolicity, of apostolic precedent. For the apostles had themselves experienced two analogous events. One was the assembly of the eleven and those with them to bring their number to twelve by casting their vote for Matthias; the other, the assembly of the twelve plus Paul and his companions, meeting in the so-called Council of Jerusalem. The first was an 'elective' assembly (to use the modern expression), the second a 'dogmatic and theological' one. In both, however, the reality enshrined in the Church's life was their authority, which, one way or another, had been seen as not exercised fully and sufficiently.

Synodical authority

Following the post-apostolic period, down through the centuries to the present day, councils of bishops have taken place. They have unswervingly relied on the dual basis which characterised the first two apostolic councils, that is, the continuation by personal link of apostolic authority in the Church, or conservation of truth in the revealed doctrine of the Church — the other, more abstract, form of ecclesiastical authority.

It is obvious that the safeguarding of authority in the Church by these episcopal synods was brought about 'in authority', according to the law of 'tautopathy' or equivalence, a principle, let it be said, which is equally valid in the sphere of ecclesiology.

The wielders of ecclesiastical authority, persuaded of their entitlement to wield it, decided what was the sole and unfailing expression and form of authority in the Church in the name of the Paraclete. It was as in the case of the assembly for the election of Matthias, and the convocation of the apostolic council. In the former case, 'they prayed and said, "Lord, who knowest the hearts of all men, show . . ."'; in the latter, 'it seemed good to the apostles and the elders, with the whole church . . . It has seemed good to the Holy Spirit and to us' (Acts 1:24; 15:22, 28).

Those were the great moments of the Church's life, when authority took wing from its initial source, the Lord, through the apostles, to the body of the Church, and most evidently to the representatives of this body, that is, the bishops, those whom the Holy Spirit has set in charge, 'to feed the church of the Lord' (Acts 20:28). All this took place in concord and harmony with the operation of the Spirit in the Church, and under his protection.

Later developments in the synod are impressive. Some of the sister Churches may be surprised by this, especially those issuing from the Reformation in the West. There were, of course, administrative rules governing the councils and, through them, the preservation of authority in the Church. Nevertheless, these councils were realities grounded theologically and ecclesiologically in the life of the Church: and they proved in most cases to be unavoidable (and thereby salutary) for preserving and affirming the revealed truth and the true faith in the Church, not only for their own times but for all times and places. Such was the case of the ecumenical councils. They were buttresses of right faith and right living for the faithful, being also concerned with their morality and customs, their social and canonical life, and so on. Of course, certain exaggerations are to be found, deviations from the proper ecclesiological norms, or bad use of them. These were either ignored or denounced by the Church. Hence the existence of such things as 'robber councils' or 'pseudo-councils'.

It will, however, be agreed that during the centuries when the councils of the one undivided Church took place, the institutionalising took place not of *one* figure of Church authority, but of *the* figure, the main bearer of this authority, and this was through the particular agency of the ecumenical councils. It was through them that the Church expressed itself and took decisions (as it still does) in all authority concerning the constancy and purity of the truth. This was and remains the greatest ecclesiological triumph and the clearest expression and objectivisation of the sense of ecclesiastical authority.

This much can be positively stated. It might, however, be useful to clarify a few details concerning actual practice.

Pluralistic tendencies

Along with the restoration of peace in the ecclesiastical world and the recognition of Christianity as the official religion of the Roman State, along too, with the unprecedented growth and multiplication of local worshipping communities and assemblies, these latter found themselves face to face with a growing number of problems, particularly theological disputes and errors. On the one hand, the authority of revelation and the teaching on church authority were threatened; on the other hand, the Church's own faith in the very function and practice of authority was weakened, inasmuch as those who were in charge were unable to reaffirm it by common agreement and decision. Councils, and most especially ecumenical councils, were the one way out of this situation.

In this sphere, however, such necessary and salutory developments were not invariably carried through with appropriate gravity, sense of responsibility and authority. The danger of the council's being secularised as an institution loomed large, as did the danger of racialism in the exercise of ecclesiastical authority, resulting either in ineffective functioning, or else in a purely juridical machine. Bad examples co-existed with the Church in close proximity. That is a well-known fact. The Roman State, and later the theocratic régime of Byzantium, various forms of both Eastern and Western civil law, a tendency in the Church to adopt secular models, the institutional and other resemblances between Church and State (such as emperor-patriarch, or senators-bishops), a weakness on the part of political leaders for dabbling in church affairs and making theological pronouncements, combined to give birth to the notorious caesaropapism and papocaesarism both in the East and West. All these factors were constant pitfalls to the life of the Church. Thus it sought to give a final form to the various types of ecclesiastical authority according to the formula endorsed by now both in the East and in the West: all the more was there need for the council as an institution, especially the ecumenical council, held in the Holy Spirit, as a legislative parliament of bishops.

Retreat from this point was impossible. The Church's practice of sending its bishops to councils, as a means of exercising the authority entrusted to it by our Lord and his apostles, became entrenched in canon law as an ecclesiastical principle. It was the ultimate point reached by truth and doctrine in a process of gradual crystallisation.

What the Church had to watch out for at such a crucial moment was a harmonious functioning between the two main coefficients in the exercise of ecclesiastical authority, that is between the actual council and the member bishops.

This needs to be stated because, together with the spread and prevalence of councils as wielders of ecclesiastical authority, a new type of bishop arose: the member-bishop, or the chairman-bishop of councils, who fostered a more vigorous type of episcopal authority, both in the councils and, fairly naturally it would seem, in the general life of the Church. There were many variations on the theme of 'episcopocentric' authority in the Church, differing from place to place, city to city, centre to centre, and finally as between East and West. It is thus that we are confronted with a *ne plus ultra* in the person and authority of the bishop of Rome, who appears bolstered by the doctrine of primacy, an extended *Magisterium Romanum*, infallibility and related circumstances in the Roman Catholic Church.

Apart from these 'Latin' exaggerations, it is a fact that in the exercise of synodical authority the place of the bishop took on added importance. When the local bishop, with his augmented authority, was a man of impeccable faith and order, this was easy to accept and even to identify with the general authority of the Church. Such were certain popes in the West. Such also were certain patriarchs in the East such as Athanasius of Alexandria, Meletius of Antioch, Gregory Nazianzen of Constantinople, Cyril of Alexandria (to mention only bishops specifically linked with the ecumenical councils). To mention yet another historical example, we need only remember the paschal quarrel dating from the correspondence between Ephesus and Rome, and how it evolved, thanks to the fortunate recognition of the bishop of Alexandria's initiative, into the well-known decision of the first Ecumenical Council of Nicaea, that the see of Alexandria alone should annually determine the date of Easter. In this case, the authority of a council and the authority of a particular bishop concurred absolutely, and this 'multidimensional' authority became ecumenically recognised by the authoritative voice of the council (in this case, an ecumenical council).

But when the authority claimed for himself by any one bishop is of doubtful worth, when it not only does not concur with, but actually contradicts the Church's authoritative doctrine and tradition, it is usually judged and condemned by the Church's authoritative conciliar voice; and so begins a terrible muddle, which casts doubt on the sense of episcopal authority in the Church's bosom. Such phenomena were not, and are not, rare in the life of the Church. It is well known that in this manner there arose an ancient line of bishops erring in their teaching on faith and dogma, who were otherwise good and irreproachable pastors. This brought about the wider issue of churches in schism, heretics and heresiarchs, those who were excommunicated — in other words, the vast problem of schism in the Church, which was and remains the most basic factor in the ecclesiological crisis of authority.

So one is led to ask: What are the criteria in this case? The erring bishop? The flock who follow him in his error? The false doctrine and tradition, as seen in each case? The surrounding worldly elements, including the only too well known exaggerations and abuses of political authority, the representative of which, as 'a bishop on the outside' (to use the historian Eusebius' expression) liked to fling himself — not always with happy results — into the theological arena?

What has proved and still proves valid in such cases? The lack of authority on the part of the party considered to be in error, or the attribution of authority to the other party condemning him? Or, beyond all these considerations, is there an objectively valid authority in the Church? If so, what? And who sets its bounds?

All these questions suggest that, for Orthodox theology, apart from authority as recognised in principle and carried out in practice, whereby the Church takes decisions in the Holy Spirit through its bishops assembled in council, especially in an ecumenical council, there are a certain number of parallel and concomitant factors surrounding and completing the sense and the function of authority in the Church. We shall list them briefly.

Parallels and points of convergence

As can be seen from the above, the whole weight of Church authority rests on the council, in particular the ecumenical council, as an institution, and on its member bishops and pastors. This is a fundamental teaching of the Orthodox Church, summed up by Professor Gerasimos Konidaris in the epigrammatic and laconic phrase: 'The chain: our Lord — apostles — bishops, safeguards the truth of the faith and the assurance of salvation'.[1]

From this basic assertion, several deductions can be made.

The collegiality of bishops

To begin with, the theme of bishops and the important role they play in exercising authority through synods, and especially ecumenical councils, deserves special treatment.

Although some bishops, as already noted, stood out above others in authority through their participation in councils, as well as sometimes outside them, they are not to be taken in isolation and individually in their capacity as spiritual leaders of a larger or smaller flock of faithful. On the contrary, they must largely be seen as part of a whole, the whole represented by the canonical episcopacy. Only when this meets together in one place, in synod, under the guidance of the Holy Spirit, to make pronouncements on matters of faith and doctrine, do the bishops exercise authority over the Church.

In other words, authority over the Church is not made up of *the bishop* but *the bishops* in the plural. With this rendering, there is no room for misunderstanding the authority wielded by the bishop as an entity. The *episcopus universalis*, who would concentrate all ecclesiastical authority in his person, does not exist in Orthodox theology, and is not even conceivable. On the other hand, authority as expressed through councils is, for the Orthodox, a *leitourgia* (function) essential to the Church, inasmuch as it is grounded on the collegiality of the Church's pastors in matters of faith and truth.

St. John Chrysostom clearly expresses this idea when describing the breadth of duties assigned to the bishop-pastor of the Church. He says that only insofar as he feels himself co-responsible for the whole Church 'throughout the *oikoumene*' is he fully a bishop.[2]

Consensus ecclesiae and consensus fidelium

Having determined the place of the bishop in the exercise of authority, the next important element to examine is the common conscience or consensus of the Church.

Though for the Orthodox Church authority properly belongs to the council, especially the ecumenical council, as the voice of the Church speaking through its bishops on matters of faith and doctrine, there is a parallel and supreme criterion of truth, and that is the consensus of the Church, which is *the unanimous consent of both clergy and laity*, the conclusive witness of the pleroma. A good general definition of this has been given by Professor Hamilcar Alivizatos.[3] Although this conclusive witness cannot be defined in organic form, notes another Orthodox theologian, Constantine Mouratidis, it is nonetheless a decisive factor in the Orthodox Church; even ecumenical councils depend on it for their recognition; hence it sets the seal of authority on questions of faith and doctrine.[4]

This means that if Orthodox Church legislation relies for its authority on the hierarchy debating in council, and the hierarchy together institutionalise authority, it is equally essential that the parallel factor of common consensus in the

Church should operate. For this provides the conclusive witness of its members on similar matters of faith and doctrine.

Professor J. Karmiris put this basic point of Orthodox theology thus:

> The pleroma, the whole body of the Church, constituted by all orthodox believers, clergy and laity, is considered in Orthodoxy to be the *agent* of infallibility in the Church, whereas the actual *voice* and *instrument* of the Church's infallibility is its supreme administrative authority, that is, the ecumenical council, in which the pleroma of the Church is represented by its bishops, who decide on matters of dogma by the grace of the Holy Spirit.[5]

So the pleroma of the Church, that is, both clergy and laity, become instruments of authority in the Church, since ecclesiologically speaking all the members of the Church are responsible for preserving the tradition of faith intact and immaculate to the end of time.

Obviously, when we speak of an agent and of a voice (or instrument) of authority in the Church, one should not conclude that these two things are different from one another, or work independently to assure ecclesiastical authority. Rather do they provide a combined witness to the same revealed truth, the same identically taught and believed truth, so that neither can ecclesiastical authority be understood without the wider conclusive witness of the consensus of believers, nor can this common consensus be understood without the authoritative organ of the Church dispensing the articles of faith.

Professor Alivizatos clarifies this dual reality by saying:

> Two things are indispensable for obtaining the common consent of the Church: firstly, a conscious effort on the part of its pastors to awaken an ecclesiastical consciousness, through doctrinal teaching which is authentic on all points, exact and free of all perversion or alteration distorting the spirit and the substance of Orthodoxy; and, secondly, once this consciousness has been awakened, vigilance over it in order to preserve a properly understood and befitting firmness in the Church.[6]

This means that the acting out of authority and the consensus of believers in the Church run parallel to one another; that at every turn the former is controlled by the latter, whilst the latter is fed and strengthened by the former, so that the Church is for ever on the watch for any deviation, pollution or error whatsoever in respect of the truth.

It follows that the consensus of the Church is not an exterior creation dictated to the members of the Church. It is, rather, the combined fruit of the faith of the whole body of believers, nurtured by the concrete action, the teaching and the preaching of the Church's *magisterium*, in harmony with the promptings of the Holy Spirit. The same Spirit, by leading men 'into all the truth' (John 16:13), renders them faithful members of the Church, having but one mind and constituting one body, under the direction of the one same Head, the sole Lord and God Jesus Christ.

Thus the consensus of the Church is a quality, not encountered in each member individually, but formed and developed in the whole body of the Church. Just as authority in the Church, wielded by the councils in the Holy Spirit, is its catholic-universal reality, so consensus is the catholic-universal function of the Church. It is a conclusive witness of the entire pleroma of the faithful to the content of truth and doctrine.

Exteriorisations of the consensus of the Church

The consensus of the Church, thus understood, exteriorises itself in the life of the Church in a large variety of ways and by using a large variety of representatives. Down the centuries, it can be seen to have acted parallel to conciliar authority, according to the different charisms of various witnesses to the faith: according to the examples of wise and willing zeal for Orthodoxy set by the holy monastic Fathers; according to the lofty theological accomplishments of a multitude of Fathers and ecclesiastical writers, who were not themselves bishops, even less members of a council; according to the forms, bonds and acts of divine worship (since *lex orandi lex credendi*); according to certain categories of inspired faithful believers, such as hermits, mystical and 'neptic' theologians, according to the life and conscientious activity of the faithful, traditionally minded members of the

Church, that is, the large bulk of the faithful, who by and large remained anonymous — and so on.

All these represented the consensus of the Church and its inherent authority. At any rate, all these localised elements surrounding the bishop and together with him made up, and still make up, that which we call a criterion of truth in the Church. Such a criterion is not to be violated, and it is irreplaceable for the exercise of authority according to Orthodox theology.

We have said that this criterion has not taken on an institutionalised aspect in the Church, and thus differs from the concrete form of ecclesiastical authority represented by the councils meeting to legislate in the Holy Spirit. But it will be admitted that the significance of the Church's common consensus is just as great (and certainly broader) than that which the hierarchy alone can provide in the absence of conclusive witness of the pleroma.

It is obvious that to analyse all these elements would take us very far.[7] In conclusion, we wish merely to say in respect of authority in the Church, that what has been said here should not be taken to mean that Orthodoxy accepts that the consensus of believers in the Church evolves free of controls and independently of a canonical organ.

This would not be very different from certain extreme views, expressed during the last century in the Slavonic milieu of Orthodox theology, notably by A. Khomiakov in his concept of *sobornost*, as well as those of some modern Orthodox theologians, in our own milieu too, who have been elaborating a theology of the laity in the Orthodox Church. The laity has a definite place in the Orthodox Church. It has also a definite role to play in the general formation of doctrine concerning the consensus of the Church, which proceeds parallel to authority in the Church.

But one should not forget the clear and classical differentiation in Orthodox theology between the agent (lit. bearer — *phoreus*) on the one hand, and the voice or instrument (*phōnē, organon*) of authority on the other. We repeat the words of Karmiris:

The pleroma of the Church, constituted by all orthodox believers, clergy and laity, is considered in Orthodoxy to be the *agent* of infallibility in the Church, whereas the actual *voice* and *instrument* of the Church's infallibility is its supreme administrative authority, that is, the ecumenical council, in which the pleroma of the Church is represented by its bishops ...[8]

Divergences between East and West

By way of conclusion, it is worth remarking on the fact that the question of authority in the Church has been put in the two worlds of Christendom which run parallel to the Orthodox, that is the Roman Catholic and the Reformed Churches in general. It was, in fact, put from the start. It has known, and still knows, a variety of fluctuations and developments. It is natural that, being a major ecclesiological topic, it should preoccupy the Orthodox in their relations with Roman Catholics and Protestants. It is not the task or responsibility of these pages to go into the details of the subject as it presents itself to those two worlds.

The absoluteness of the relevant Roman Catholic doctrine, as expressed in the overall theology of the *Magisterium Romanum*, and as put into action in its main ecclesiological structures, particularly in the papal primacy, papal infallibility and general papal authority in the West is the very touchstone of relations between Orthodoxy and Roman Catholicism. It is the main point of discussion in the new theological dialogue between them, and it will brook no delay.

As for the Reformed world, and the Churches issuing from the Reformation, it is well known that from the Orthodox point of view the question of authority in the Church is not only considered as an absolutely critical point of dialogue, but it also stands out as a condition of entering into theological dialogue with them.

How ecclesiastical authority is to be envisaged, by what ecclesiastical structure or organ it is exercised and in what manner, how binding this authority is on all the members of the Church — these are the basic points which the Orthodox Church is usually anxious to clarify. For it considers them to be *sine qua non* factors of any substantial dialogue.

NOTES

1. G. Konidaris, 'Hē spoudaiotēs tōn peri to politeuma tēs archegonou ekklēsias ereunōn dia tēn Oikoumenikēn Kinēsin meta stoicheiōn tēs lyseōs' in *Eucharistērion tō Didaskalō Ham. Alivizatō* (Athens 1958), p. 195.
2. *In S. Eustathium Antiochenum* 3 (*PG* 50, 602).
3. Ham. Alivizatos, 'Hē koinē syneidēsis tēs Ekklēsias' in *Epistēmonikē Epetēris tēs Theologikēs Scholēs tou Panepistēmiou Athēnōn* (Athens 1955), p. 28.
4. C. Mouratidis, *Hē ousia kai to politeuma tēs Ekklēsias* (Athens 1958), p. 17.
5. J. Karmiris, *Synopsis tēs Dogmatikēs Didaskalias tēs Orthodoxou Katholikēs Ekklēsias* (Athens 1957), pp. 7ff.
6. Ham. Alivisatos, art. cit., p. 38.
7. Ch. Konstantinidis, Metropolitan of Myra, *Basika tina peri Hieras Paradoseōs* (Athens 1978), pp. 35ff and pp. 42ff.
8. Karmiris, *Synopsis*, loc. cit.

THIRD CONSULTATION

Geneva

March 6-11, 1983

CHAPTER 5

THE TRINITARIAN FOUNDATION AND CHARACTER OF FAITH AND OF AUTHORITY IN THE CHURCH

THOMAS F. TORRANCE

The Trinitarian Perspective

This essay presupposes the Orthodox Doctrine of the Holy Trinity, *mia ousia, treis hypostaseis*, in accordance particularly with the teaching of Athanasius, Gregory Nazianzen, Cyril of Alexandria and as summarised in the eighth century document *De sacrosancta Trinitate* attributed to Cyril of Alexandria and incorporated in the *De fide orthodoxa* of John of Damascus. This is the doctrine of the Holy Trinity which came to expression in the great credal and conciliar statements of the Church which operated not with formalised definitions but with ways of thinking within the limits set by God's self-revelation, from the Father, through the Son and in the Holy Spirit, and as mediated to the Church from the Apostles. In line with the stress of Athanasius and Gregory Nazianzen the theological terms used, such as *ousia, hypostasis, pēgē, archē, aitia*, are applied to God in such a way that they are stretched beyond their ordinary sense and reference and are recognised when they are employed in this way to be governed by the self-revelation of God in such a way that they are made to indicate more than as human terms they can naturally specify. This means that we must take care that the natural images and analogies which this human language carries are not read back into God but are critically controlled by the self-revelation of God which they are employed to articulate. Since it is not the theological terms themselves that are important but the divine realities they signify, they have to be employed and interpreted in a flexible, elastic and dynamic way under the power of the mystery of the Holy Trinity, and therefore in a reverent and godly way (*kat' eulabeian, kat' eusebeian*), and in accordance with the nature of God (*kata physin theou*) as he has graciously made himself known to us through his economic condescension (*oikonomikē sygkatabasis*) in the Incarnation.

We could not think of God, far less speak of him, as triune *in himself* as well as in his self-revelation to us through his saving and reconciling acts in history, were it not for the fact that through the Son and in the Spirit the Father has given us access (*prosagōgē*) to himself (Epesians 2:18), in such a way that we know the Father, the Son and the Holy Spirit to be one in operation (*energeia*) and one in being (*ousia*), while nevertheless distinct in their persons (*hypostaseis*) as Father, Son and Holy Spirit. This does not mean of course that we can now comprehend (*katalabein*) God or grasp what God is (*ti esti theos*), for it is quite impossible for us to get behind the being of God and seize it with our minds. But it does mean that God who is ultimately ineffable, surpassing all created being (*ousia hyperousios*), has incomprehensibly made himself personally and intimately accessible to us in Jesus Christ within the conditions of our human existence in space and time in a way that is utterly faithful to and consistent with what God eternally is in himself. Through the incarnate Son and in the mission of the Spirit a way has been opened up for us to the Father, so that we may know God in some real measure as he is in himself, since the Son and the Spirit are proper to God and dwell eternally in the one Being of God. Through the Son of God who is *homoousios* with the Father we may know God in his own inherent *Logos* or Intelligibility, and in the Spirit who is *homoousios* with the Father and the Son our knowing of God really is knowing of God as he is in himself, since through participating in the Spirit we are made partakers of God himself. Thus through the Son and in the Spirit who eternally inhere in the being (*enousioi*) of God, our knowledge of God is grounded in and controlled by what God is in himself as Father, Son and Holy Spirit — that is, in God as one *ousia*, described and worshipped in three perfect objective *hypostaseis*, coeternal in power, glory and authority wholly coinhering in one another, who are inconfusedly united and inseparably distinguished as Father, Son and Holy Spirit. As Cyril of Alexandria tersely expressed it: This is 'God conceived in a holy and consubstantial Trinity' (*Comm. on John* 15.1).

No one insisted more than Athanasius that the only worthy and lawful doctrine of God is that reached under the constraint of his revealed nature as 'One Holy Trinity' when knowledge of God and worship of God merge into one another. We cannot know God in accordance with his divine nature except in a godly way, that is, in such a way that we are restrained by the sheer Holiness and Majesty of the divine being from transgressing the bounds of our creaturely being in inquiring beyond what is given through the Son and received by the Spirit, and therefore from thinking presumptuously and illegitimately of God. Before the transcendent intelligibility and ineffability of the Godhead we veil our faces like the cherubim, and faith and a godly and reverent use of reason together with worship, wonder and silence inform the movement of our understanding toward the Father through the Son and in the Spirit answering to the movement of God's grace from the Father, through the Son and in the Spirit toward us (*Ad Serapionem*, 1. 15–20, 24; 4. 2-7). It is not surprising that Athanasius could claim that the knowledge of the Holy Trinity approached in this way is what *theology* in the most proper sense means. '*Theologia* is perfect in the Trinity, and this is the true and only *theosebeia*.' (*Con. Arianos*, 1. 18).

While the doctrine of the Holy Trinity derived from the self-revelation of God the Father through the Son and in the Spirit, and took shape through a faithful interpretation of the Holy Scriptures within the framework of the Apostolic tradition, it was with the Councils of Nicaea and Constantinople that it was irreversibly built into the mind of the Church. Thus through the Nicene-Constantinopolitan Creed it became clear that the doctrine of the Trinity constitutes the foundation of the Church's faith and provides it with its inherent controlling structure. The unity and community of being and operation within the Holy Trinity and in all the economic acts of the Holy Trinity toward us and for our sake in revelation and salvation, which gave rise to the Church as the communion of people in the world concorporate with Christ, means that all the doctrines of the Church's faith are basically trinitarian in their character and pattern: they take their essential truth and form from the consubstantial communion of Father, Son and Holy Spirit in the one indivisible Trinity. That is the framework within which we must seek to elucidate the intrinsic structure of the faith and the nature of authority in the Church.

It may help us at this point to say two things about that trinitarian framework in respect of the way in which we allow it to direct our thought.

1. The Church derives from the eternal purpose of God to create human beings and share with them the life and love which God has within himself as Father, Son and Holy Spirit. It is rooted in the Incarnation of the Son of God, for in him the love of God has overflowed into the world and embodied itself in our humanity, and it is maintained through the operation of the Spirit who unites it in body and spirit to Christ and makes it participate in the divine nature. Thus the mystery of the Church is grounded in a three-fold communion. Antecedent to all is the eternal Communion of the Father, Son and Holy Spirit, that is, the Love that God is eternally in himself, the consubstantial Communion of the Father, the Son and the Holy Spirit. That Love of God has been poured out for us and embodied in Jesus Christ, the Beloved Son, in whom by the operation of the Holy Spirit divine nature and human nature were uniquely and hypostatically united in one Person. It is that same Love mediated by the atonement which is poured out by the Spirit within the Church, for through the Communion of the Spirit the Church partakes of the oneness of the Father and the Son in Jesus Christ, and is constituted itself the Community of Love on earth in whose midst God himself dwells. Because God is Love, the pouring out of his Love upon man is the pouring out of the divine Life. The participation of the Church in that divine Life, which it is given through the Communion of the Spirit, is its supernatural life, which it lives from age to age only as it is grounded in the measureless Love of God. Thus the Communion of the Father, the Son and the Holy Spirit has wonderfully overflowed into our humanity in the Incarnation, taking unique form in the hypostatic union and reconciliation wrought out in Jesus Christ, and through the Communion of the Spirit flows over from him into history in the life and mission of the Church. This means that we must allow the nature of the consubstantial communion in the Holy Trinity, as far as that is revealed to us, to govern what we are to think and say about the

canon of truth and authority in the Church as exhibited in the
Nicene-Constantinopolitan Creed.

2. The fact that God the Father has communicated himself to
us in this trinitarian way through the incarnate economy of his
Son, the Word made flesh in Jesus Christ, means that the
incarnate Son constitutes the real focus of the doctrine of the
Trinity, and the regulative centre with reference to which all the
worship, faith and mission of the Church take their shape: from
the Father, through the Son and in the Spirit, and to the Father,
through the Son and in the Spirit. Since it is from the Son, the
Logos of God incarnate, that we take our knowledge of the
Father and of the Spirit, as Athanasius made so indubitably
clear in his *Epistles to Serapion*, and since there is a mutual relation
of knowing and being and operation between the Son and the
Father, it is specifically from the consubstantial relation
between the Son and the Father that we must take our basic cue
and allow it to have regulative force in all we have to think of the
Church as the Body of Christ, the earthly-historical form of his
existence in the world, and everything we have to think and
formulate about its institutional life, order and authority in the
fulfilment of its service and mission in the Gospel. If we have a
wrong conception of the relation of the Son to the Father, then
everything else in our understanding of the Gospel and the
ordering of its life and mission in the world will inevitably go
wrong. But if we allow the consubstantial relation of the Son to
the Father to govern our understanding of the Faith throughout
the three-levelled dimension of Trinitarian Communion in God,
in Christ, and in the Church, then we should be able to arrive at
an account of our specific theme which may command a real
measure of assent from Orthodox and Reformed alike.

Moreover, if we bear constantly in mind the ineffability of the
Holy Trinity which sets a limit to what we may know and
express of God's inner coinherent relations as Father, Son and
Holy Spirit, to which we have no creaturely analogy, we will not
allow ourselves to transgress the bounds (*horoi*) which the
Trinitarian Communion imposes upon what we may declare
about truth and authority in the Church, which reflect but fall
infinitely short of the Truth and Authority of God himself. We
would thus be following the godly restraint of the Nicene
Fathers who, as Athanasius reported, in a careful and precise

declaration of the substance of the Faith in accordance with the mind (*phronēma*) of the Apostles, did not lay down formal decrees like imperial edicts, which for them would have been lacking in *eusebeia* before God, but wrote 'Thus believes the Catholic Church' and then 'confessed how they believed' (*pōs pisteuousin* — *De Synodis*, 3-5). At the same time, however, the Nicene Fathers indicated how the terms they used (e.g. *homoousios tō patri*) were to be understood by marking the 'boundaries' (*ta horisthenta*) of their confession which could not be transgressed without lapse into error. Hence they drew up a number of 'canons' or negative delimitations which they appended to their credal declaration to guard it from misunderstanding and heretical distortion. They drew a limit (*horos*) beyond which in *eulabeia* and *eusebeia* they could not go, declining to reduce the ineffable mystery of God, Father, Son and Holy Spirit, and the economic acts of the Holy Trinity, to fixed dogmatic definitions, and in a doxological confession of faith characterised by an open semantic focus (*skopos*) toward the unlimited Reality and Transcendent Majesty of God, they offered an evangelical declaration of what they found themselves obliged to affirm under the constraint of divine revelation mediated to them through the Holy Scriptures. At the same time they deemed it necessary to expose the perversity of heresy and thereby 'show the mind of the truth for the security of the faithful'. That is the way in which Athanasius himself viewed the work of the Nicene Council (*Con. Arianos*, 3. 1) and so described the credal statements formulated by the Council as *ta horisthenta* (wrongly translated in Latin by *decreta* in the title of his work on the Nicene Council, *De decretis*).

In this light we may now turn back to the key-concept, *the relation of the Son to the Father*, upon which, as the sustained debates of the fourth century from the Council of Nicaea in 325 to the first Council of Constantinople in 381 steadily brought home to the Church, everything ultimately depends. Following the lead of Athanasius in which, as Gregory Nazianzen put it, 'he kept within the bounds of godliness' (*en horois meinas tēs eusebeias, Oratio* xxi. 13), the Church taught that Sonship and Fatherhood in God are proper to each other and belong inseparably and eternally together in the one Holy Trinity. In disparaging the words of our Lord, 'I in the Father and the

Father in me' (John 14:10), Asterius had asked the ungodly questions: 'How can the one be contained in the other and the other in the one?' and 'How at all can the Father who is greater be contained in the Son who is less?'. In reply Athanasius put forward the doctrine later known as *perichorēsis* which expresses the fact that the Father and the Son are each whole and perfect God, that they are in each other because their being is one and the same, and that they are perfect and have one being, for the second Person is properly and inherently the Son of the First Person and is no less very God than he — that is, the Father and the Son perfectly and mutually 'contain' one another (*Con. Arianos*, 3. 1ff; cf. *De synodis*, 15, 26). This applies of course equally to the Holy Spirit (*Con. Arianos*, 1. 47f, 50, 56; 2. 18; 3. 15, 24f, 44; *De decretis*, 26; *Ad Serapionem, passim*). The points that are of immediate relevance to our discussion are these: (*a*) Since the whole being of the Son is proper to the being of the Father and 'the very Form (*eidos*) and Godhead of the Father is the being of the Son', the Sonship of the Son falls *within* and not outside the Godhead. (*b*) Since the Son and the Father are one indivisible God, all that the Son and the Father are and have is in common, so that there is no greater or less, no inequality in God, the very *same things* are said of the Son that are said of the Father, except his being said to be Father (*Con. Arianos*, 3. 3-6; *De synodis*, 48-51).

That is to say, he who became incarnate in Jesus Christ is none other than the Son of God whose relation to the Father is *internal* to his being and nature as God, and who, as fully and perfectly God in his nature, has full and perfect *equality* with the Father within the union and communion of the Holy Trinity (Athanasius, *Con. Arianos*, 3. 60ff). Hence everything we say of Jesus Christ the incarnate Son of the Father must be governed by his internal relation to the Father and his equality with the Father. As God of God, very God of very God, he is in his own Person the very Truth (*Autoalētheia*) and the very Authority (*Autoexousia*) of the one Holy Trinity. The importance of this understanding of the relation of the Son to the Father may be brought out by setting over against it the positions adopted by the Arians and semi-Arians, and pointing out the consequences of their views for our theme.

(*a*) Owing to a radical dualism in their underlying framework of thought, the Arians drew a sharp line of demarcation between the being of the Son and the being of the Father, and thus offered an account of Jesus Christ solely in terms of his external, moral relations with God and not in terms of his internal, ontic relations with him. This affected everything the Arians had to say about the Gospel and about the Church, for by detaching the teaching and the work of Christ from his Person they demoted Christ himself from central significance in the faith. Consequently the work of Christ was expounded only in terms of his external, moral relations with mankind and not in terms of any internal, ontic relation with what, as God himself become man, he had assumed from us in our alienated condition in order to effect salvation and healing in the depths of our human being. Moreover, the Church was not regarded as being ontically united to Christ as his Body through union and communion with him, but as no more than a community of people externally united through the pursuit of common moral ideals. It was inevitable that such a thoroughly dualist and moralist approach to Christ and the Gospel should seriously affect the basic concept of truth in the Arians' understanding of divine revelation and in the faith of the Church, replacing 'theology' by 'mythology', thereby laying the Church open to the impact of secular culture and worldly institutions. This is precisely what happened in Constantinople during the forty years of Arian dominance before the first Council of Constantinople, as we learn from the epistles and songs as well as the orations of Gregory of Nazianzen.

(b) The semi-Arians, taking their cue from Origen and Plotinus, held a doctrine of the Trinity in which they regarded the Son as eternally generated from the will of the Father — which was not in principle different from the way in which they thought of the created universe as deriving from the will of the *Pantokratōr* and yet as eternally coexisting with him. Thus they introduced a subordinationist principle into the Trinity, differentiating the Monarchy of the Father from the eternally caused Deities of the Son and the Spirit. The effect of this was to throw up a hierarchical concept of the Trinity in accordance with which Jesus Christ was not regarded as intrinsically the Truth and Authority of God, God in his own being as God incarnate, i.e., as *Autoalētheia* and *Autoexousia*, but as the Bearer of the Truth and Authority of God in a secondary, delegated way. This concept of a hierarchy of authority within the Trinity not only opened the way for, but was appealed to in justification for, the assimilation of the institutional structure of the Church to the secular patterns of hierarchical authority exhibited by Byzantium and Rome, thereby gravely damaging the biblical and apostolic concept of authority in the Church derived through union and communion with Christ.

It is with reference to his valiant attempts to defend and rehabilitate Nicene theology in face of the positions adopted by Arians and semi-Arians that we are to appreciate the five great 'Theological Orations' delivered by Gregory Nazianzen in Constantinople in 380 A.D. In line with the teaching of the other Cappadocians, Basil, Gregory Nyssen and Amphilochius, he sought to develop the trinitarian theology of Athanasius by giving more precise exposition of *mia ousia, treis hypostaseis* that would meet and counter the arguments of Eunomius. The general Cappadocian view, however, seemed to import a modification of Athanasius' position in a way that clearly made Gregory Nazianzen uneasy. This seemed to imply a partial return to the Origenist notion that the Godhead is complete primarily in the Father alone, but mediately in the Son and the Spirit through their origination from the Father, against which Athanasius had insisted on the perfect equality of the Father, Son and Holy Spirit, in each of whom the Godhead is complete. Athanasius thought of the generation of the Son from the Being of God as a generation 'by nature' (*physei*), and not by will except in the sense that in God will and nature are one and the same; and therefore of the Son as generated by the Father in a way that transcends any distinction between free will and necessity but in a way in which the Son is identical with the eternal will of the Father, fully coequal as well as consubstantial and coeternal with him (*Con. Arianos*, 3. 60, 66). Gregory, on the other hand, in his eagerness to safeguard the one only God by referring the Son and the Spirit to one *pēgē, archē, aitia*, thought of the Son as eternally caused by the Father's will (although in a quite ineffable way in that God's will and action coincide) which made him think of the Father as 'greater' (*meizōn*) than the Son, although this did not mean, Gregory claimed, that the Father is greater in being than the Son, for both the Son and the Spirit are of one and the same Being as the Father and coeternal with him (*Oratio*, 29 (3). 3, 15; 30 (4). 7; 31 (5). 14; cf. 20. 7, 10, 29; 25. 15; 40. 43, etc.). What worried Gregory Nazianzen was the combination of the terms *archē* and *aitia* in speaking of the 'origin' of the Son, for it appeared to import 'superiority' and 'inferiority' in the Trinity (*Oratio*, 40. 41, 43) which conflicted with his own basic convictions (*Oratio*, 21. 10; 31 (5). 14; 40. 41, 43; 42. 15f; 43. 30). There is clearly an unresolved ambiguity in Gregory's thought, due to his persistent stress upon the fact that God the Father is the cause (*aitios, aitia*) of the Son which he felt necessary to avoid the pagan notion of three ultimate principles or *archai* (*Oratio*, 20. 7; 21. 10, 34; 29 (3). 3, 15, 19; 31 (5). 14, 30, 33). Athanasius could on occasion speak of the Father as *aitios* of the Son precisely as *Father* of the Son, but in that sense only, not because he caused the Son. But he went on to insist, as we have seen, that all that is said of the Father is said of the Son, except 'Father', for there is complete equality between the Father and the Son (*Con. Arianos*, 2. 54; *De synodis*, 36f, 49). In contrast to this Gregory could claim that 'all that the Father has, belongs to the Son, except causality' (*Oratio*, 34. 8, 10; cf. 30. 11), although he could also speak of the difference between the Son and the Father as one of 'relation' (*schesis*) (*Oratio*, 29(3). 16; 30 (4). 20; 31 (5). 19). Whenever Athanasius referred to the words of Jesus 'The Father is greater (*meizōn*) than I' (John 14. 28), and similar expressions such as those about the 'servant' reflecting the humble condition of the Son, he interpreted them *soteriologically* in terms of the incarnate economy or the economic condescension of the Son (see for example the sustained discussion in *Con. Arianos*, 1. 37-64). Gregory could do the same (*Oratio*, 30 (4). 3ff) but curiously not with reference to John 14. 28.

It is highly significant that when Cyril of Alexandria turned back to the teaching of Athanasius, rejecting like him all idea of a hierarchy in God, while accepting the Cappadocian formula, *mia ousia, treis hypostaseis*, he eliminated the ambiguity that had arisen, by rejecting the notion of causal relations within the Trinity as quite unbiblical (*Thesaurus* MPG 75, 125, 128, 144f; *Dialogus* II, MPG 75, 744f; cf. 721 and 769; *Comm. on John* 14. 28). It is 'only economically' (*oikonomikōs*) that we may speak of the Father as 'greater' than the Son (*Thesaurus*, MPG 75, 144). Here we have the full orthodox doctrine of the *Holy Trinity in one*

Godhead, One God in three Persons, in which the Persons are understood as wholly coinhering in one another, as completely coequal and coeternal as well as consubstantial, with one authority, glory, power, will, activity and goodness, and who as such are *one arche*, as Athanasius had claimed (*Ad Antiochenos*, 5). This was wholly consistent with the statement of Gregory Nazianzen, 'When I say *God*, I mean Father, Son and Holy Spirit' (*Oratio*, 38. 8; 45. 4). Since that one God in the unity and community of the Holy Trinity was at work in the Incarnation, it is to the incarnate *Eidos* of the Godhead in Jesus Christ, that is to the relation of the Holy Trinity to the humanity of the Son, that must look for the Truth, 'the pure seal and unerring imprint of the Father', as Gregory called it (*Oratio*, 30 (4). 20), upon which the Faith of the Church and Authority in the Church rest — and not to some supposed hierarchical principle in God. We must now try to spell this out in the second part of this essay.

We have seen that Jesus Christ constitutes the creative ground and controlling centre of the Church's faith and life, for it is from him that we take our knowledge of the Father and of the Spirit, and therefore of the Holy Trinity, and from him that we take our knowledge of the Gospel and the Church and derive all our faith and life, for in him the mystery (*mysterion*) of God himself has been embodied and set forth. In the New Testament *mysterion* refers primarily to the union of God and man eternally purposed in God and now revealed and set forth in Jesus Christ as true God and true Man in one Person, a union which creates room for itself in the midst of our estranged humanity and through communion (*koinonia*) gathers human beings into one Body with Jesus Christ. In Jesus Christ that union has, as it were, been thrust like an axis into the midst of our humanity, making everything revolve around it and have significance only in relation to it. That axis directs us back into the eternal life and communion of the Holy Trinity, but it also manifests itself in history in the Church of Jesus Christ. Jesus Christ is himself the manifestation, the realisation, of the eternal purpose of God, and it is in *koinonia* with the mystery he embodies, and through participation (*koinonein*) in the divine purpose, that the Church of Christ is called into being and maintained from age to age as the appointed 'place' (*chōra*) where Christ continues to make himself known, as the community (*koinonia*) in which he dwells by his Word and Spirit, and which he who has ascended to fill all things will bring to its fulness in his redeeming purpose, for he, the Head of all creation, of realities visible and invisible, will return again to consummate his purpose of love in the new creation. Then the mystery already consummated in Christ, and in which the Church even now has *koinonia*, will be fully revealed and manifested in the new heaven and new earth. It is significant that in the New Testament the term *koinonia* has a double reference: primarily it refers to participation through the Spirit in Jesus Christ, participation in the union of God and man in him, and through him in the Holy Trinity, but secondarily it refers to the fellowship or community which is the Church, the communion which exists between the members of the Body of Christ through concorporate union with Christ — though neither sense may be separated from the other. That is the Church-constituting *koinonia tou mysteriou Christou*, which is to be traced back to the mystery of the eternal communion of Love which God is as Father, Son and Holy Spirit and forward to the revelation of the mystery of God's Love in the final consummation of all things.

Since Jesus Christ is himself the Alpha and Omega of that unlimited range of God's purpose in creation and redemption, we must keep our thought as close to him as possible in his incarnate reality as God and Man hypostatically united without confusion and without separation in one Person. In him as the incarnate *Ego Eimi* of God himself, Person, Word and Act are uniquely and indivisibly one, interpenetrating and coinhering in one another. Thus Jesus Christ meets us as One whose Word and whose Act coincide with the living reality of his Person, and whose Person is not other than his Word or his Act, for his Person is intrinsically Word and Act, while his Word and Act are never impersonal but always intrinsically personal. He is in Person identical with his Word, his Word is itself his Act, and his Act is the power of his Person. In Jesus Christ, then, we have to do with the *Autoalētheia* and the *Autoexousia* embodied in his own Person in such a way that the Truth and Authority of God concentrated in Jesus Christ function only in and through the inherent nity of his Person, Word and Act, and therefore only in an intensely personal and personalising way. That is how we find *Autoalētheia* and *Autoexousia* functioning in the faith and life of the Church as it took its rise from the Apostolic Nucleus which Christ united so closely with himself, making it the foundation upon which he built his Church and in which he embodied his Truth and Authority in such a way through communion with himself that throughout all its mission and expansion in the world he continues himself, to be the *Archē* of all God's ways and works, the ultimate *Judge* of all truth and falsity in the Church's understanding and proclamation of the Faith, and the ultimate *Lord* over all ministry and structure in the institutional existence and development of the Church. While *Autoalētheia* and *Autoexousia* cannot really be separated, we shall consider first *Autoalētheia* in the Faith of the Church, and then *Autoexousia* in the Life of the Church.

Autoalētheia in the Faith of the Church

In the New Testament the Gospel refers not merely to the good news about salvation but to Jesus Christ who in his own Person, Word and Act is the very core of the Gospel — i.e., to what John Calvin spoke of as 'Christ clothed with his Gospel'. Thus the *kērygma* refers not merely to proclamation about Christ but to the Reality proclaimed, Jesus Christ who is personally, actively and savingly at work through the *kērygma*. That is to say, *kērygma* has an essentially objective and concrete sense, Christ proclaiming himself and embodying his self-proclamation in the proclamation of the Apostles. The same approach must be adopted to the cognate term *baptisma* which cannot be identified with the rite of Baptism, i.e. *baptismos* (a term the NT does not use of Christian Baptism), but refers primarily to the vicarious Baptism with which Christ himself was baptised and which is the ground of our Baptism into him through the Spirit. Likewise we must interpret what the New Testament has to say about 'the Faith once delivered to the saints' (Jude 3) which refers to the original objective *datum* of divine Revelation in Jesus Christ and his Gospel upon which the very existence of the Church as the Body of Christ in the world depended, and which exercised a regulative force in all its witness, preaching and teaching. The Apostolic Church regarded itself as entrusted with a sacred deposit (*parathēkē, parakatathēkē, depositum*) enshrined in the Apostolic Foundation of the Church laid by Christ himself and livingly empowered through his indwelling Spirit of Truth, which the Church was bound to guard inviolate in contending for the Faith, and for which it had to render an account before God (1 Tim. 4:6, 6:20; 2 Tim. 1.12-14, 2:2, 4, 4:3; Titus 1:9, 13; cf. 2 Thess. 2:15, 3:6; Gal. 1:9, 2:2, 9; 1 Cor. 11:23, 15.3; 2 Cor. 11:3-4; Rom. 7:7; Hebrews 3:1, 4:14, 10:23). In the last analysis 'the Deposit of Faith' is to be understood as the whole living Fact of Christ and his saving Acts in the indivisible unity of his Person, Word and Life, as through the Resurrection and Pentecost he fulfilled and unfolded the content of his self-revelation as Saviour and Lord within his Church. We do not have to do here with Christ apart from his Word or with the Word apart from Christ, nor with Christ apart from his Truth or with the Truth apart from Christ, for he is the incarnate embodiment of the Word and Truth of God in his own personal Being, who continues in the power of his resurrection to make his mighty Acts of redemption effective in the life and faith of all who are baptised in his Name and who draw near to the Father through his atoning sacrifice and in the one Spirit whom the Father sends in the Name of the Son.

From the perspective of the Acts of the Apostles we are concerned here with the living and dynamic *Word* which was at work in the foundation and growth of the Church (Acts 6:7, 12:24, 19:20; cf. Col. 1:5-6), communicating himself through the Spirit in the witness and preaching of the Apostles, letting his self-revelation take definitive shape in the Apostolic mind and embody itself in the Apostolic mission, in such a way that the identity and continuity of the Church and its teaching in history became inseparably bound up with it (cf. Rom. 6:17). This does not mean that Christ the Word was resolved into the Apostolic Word, nor therefore that the Deposit of Faith may be identified as such with the preaching and teaching of the Apostles, for it continues to remain identical with the incarnate self-communication of God in Jesus Christ mediated after the Ascension and Pentecost through the Apostles. It does mean, however, that from that time onward people may have access to the Deposit of Faith only in the form which, under the creative impact of the risen Lord and his Spirit, it has assumed once and for all in the Apostolic Tradition, i.e., through the Apostolic preaching and interpretation of the Gospel mediated to us in the

Scriptures of the New Testament and through baptismal incorporation into Christ in the midst of his Church, where he continues to make himself known from faith to faith and to be savingly at work in the power of his indwelling Spirit.

That was how the original Christians regarded the Deposit of Faith, as finally inseparable from the very substance of the Gospel, the revealing and saving Event of Christ crucified, risen and glorified, but once for all entrusted to the Church through its Apostolic Foundation informing and structuring its life and faith as the Body of Christ. This was something which the Church had to treasure above all else, guarding it intact against all misunderstanding and serving its faithful transmission to future generations through divinely appointed ordinances binding the Church in every age to its Apostolic Foundation in Christ as the ground of its continuity and renewal in history. While the Deposit of Faith was replete with the Truth as it is in Jesus, embodying didactic, kerygmatic and theological material, by its very nature it could not be resolved into a system of truths or a set of normative doctrines and formulated beliefs, for the truths, doctrines and beliefs entailed could not be abstracted from the embodied form they were given in Christ, and given by Christ in the Apostolic Foundation of the Church, without loss of their real substance. Nevertheless in this embodied form 'the Faith once delivered to the saints' constituted the regulative basis for all explicit formulation of Christian truth, doctrine and belief in the deepening under-standing of the Church and its regular instruction of catechu-mens and the faithful.

It is with Irenaeus in the middle of the second century that we find the most enlightening account of the Deposit of Faith in which he drew out the implications of the Apostolic and Biblical teaching in the context of sustained refutation of Gnostic heresies. With him the pattern inherent in the Evangelical content of the Faith and the Apostolic tradition of the Faith began to be unfolded in a way that clearly influenced later developments in the East as well as the West, not least those that led to the Nicene Creed.

It is highly significant that Irenaeus operated with a concept of *embodied truth* or *embodied doctrine*, for the theological foundation of the Faith and its empirical or historical foundation were

identical in the saving revelation and intervention of God
fulfilled once for all in Jesus Christ (Acts 4:11-12; 1 Cor. 3:11;
Ephesians 2:20-2). It was the indivisible reality and wholeness of
the Truth embodied in Jesus Christ that constituted the
fundamental theological basis or canon of truth in all Irenaeus'
efforts to be faithful to the sacred Deposit of Faith in expounding
and defending the Gospel. At that basic level the Person of
Christ as Saviour, his saving Acts, and his Message of salvation
are to be understood as ultimately one and the same, for they
coinhere inseparably in one another. That is to say, in Christ
Jesus event and message, fact and meaning, the Word and the
word, the Truth and truths, are all intrinsically integrated and
cannot be torn apart without serious dismemberment and
distortion of the Faith. What Christ has done for us and
proclaimed to us he has embodied in his own personal Reality,
and is, and what he is in his own Person he continues to be as Act
of God for us and Word of God to us. As the Word of God, by
whom all things visible and invisible were created, himself
become incarnate for our sake, Christ is also the Word who in
being proclaimed to us remains the mighty saving Act of God
(*Adv. haer.* 3.9-11, edit. by W. H. Harvey, vol. II, pp. 30-6;
Epideixis, passim). Thus the message of Christ must be regarded
as more than the message of who he was and what he has done,
for it is itself the saving power of God constantly at work among
people, and effectively operative in the faith of the Church,
anchoring it and giving it substance in what he has done and
ever is as Saviour and Lord in the fulfilment of the covenant
promises of God to mankind.

It is because it is interlocked with the truth and constancy or
'faith' of God in Christ and with the economy of redemption
fulfilled through his Incarnation, that the Faith which the
Church has received from the Apostolic 'depository' and
through the Apostolic Tradition in the Scriptures, remains
always and everywhere 'one and the same' (*una et eadem fides*)
without abstraction or addition. It does not deviate from the
original *kērygma* of the truth and keeps on shining and
enlightening all who are ready to come to knowledge of it (*Adv.
haer.* 1.3, vol. I, p. 94; 3.1-4, vol. II, pp. 1-18; 3.11.1, vol. II, p.
47; cf. 3.12.9, vol. II, p. 62; 4.4ff, vol. II, pp. 234ff; and 5.20, vol.
II, pp. 377ff). It is very understandable that Irenaeus should lay

such stress upon the actual empirical or historical relation to the Truth in the concrete form in which it was entrusted to the Apostolic Church by the Holy Spirit. But it is also understandable that, since the Truth is 'the sure gift of the Spirit' (*charisma veritatis certum*), he should lay such stress upon the self-sustaining and self-explicating nature of the Truth in its identity with the living Christ who in his saving work and Person *is* the Truth, for as such it constitutes 'the charismatic principle' of the Church's renewal and continuity in history (*Adv. haer.* 4.40.2, vol. II, p. 236). Thus regarded, the Deposit of Faith in which that living Truth is embodied in the Church is what Irenaeus in a famous passage spoke of as 'the deposit which by the Spirit of God always rejuvenates itself and rejuvenates the vessel in which it is lodged' (*depositum juvenescens et juvenescere faciens*, *Adv. haer.* 3.38.1, vol. II, p. 131; cf. *sola vera et vivifica fides*, *Adv. haer.* 3. Pref. and 3, vol. II, pp. 1 & 12). That does not take place, however, except through constant reference back to the Apostolic ground of the Church and to the truth embedded in it, for the Faith with which the Church in all ages is entrusted as the principle of its renewal and canon of its understanding of the Gospel is that which has been once for all delivered to the saints as the unalterable foundation laid for it by Christ in himself and in his Apostles (*Adv. haer.* 3.1-5, vol. II, pp. 2-28). It is in this light that the historical tradition (*paradosis*) of the Faith, and the historical succession (*diadochē*) of presbyters and bishops from the original Apostles, through which the integrity of that tradition of the Faith is to be checked, is to be understood. But no less important for Irenaeus was the stress upon the empirical tradition and living reception of the Faith through the ordinance of Baptism in the context of the worship of God, meditation upon the Holy Scriptures and instruction in the Gospel when salvation was written in the hearts of the faithful by the Spirit. In this context 'the tradition', 'the *kērygma* of the truth', and 'the canon of truth' were all treated as operative equivalents with only differing emphases (*Adv. haer.* 1.1.20, vol. I, p. 87f; 1.15, p. 188; 2.8.1, p. 272; 2.40.1-41.3, pp. 347-52; 3.1-5, vol. II, pp. 2-20; 3.11.7, p. 41; 3.12.6-7, pp. 58f; 3.15.1, p. 79; 3.38.1-2, pp. 131f; 4.57.2, 4, pp. 274-6; 5. Pref., pp. 313f; 5.20.1-2, pp. 377-80; and *Epideixis*).

There is another feature of the Deposit of Faith which was of special importance for Irenaeus, the fact that 'the body of truth' which constituted the theological content of the Deposit was characterised by an intrinsic order or structure reflecting the economic design of the self-revelation of God the Father through the Son and the Holy Spirit. It is by uncovering the internal structure of the Faith and bringing into clear relief the essential arrangement of 'the body of truth and the harmonious adaptation of its members', that the Deposit of Faith can be used both as an instrument of inquiry in the interpretation of the Holy Scriptures and as a canon of truth enabling the Church to offer a clear demonstration of the Apostolic *kērygma* whereby it can be distinguished from all heretical deviations and distortions and shine forth in its own self-evidence (*Adv. haer.* 1.19-20, vol. I, pp. 80-90; 2.37-43, pp. 342-58; 3.12.11, vol. II, p. 65; 3.38, pp. 13f; *Epideixis*, 1-6).

As Irenaeus shows us, it was when the Church was engaged in clarifying its grasp of the doctrinal substance of the Faith in this way, in the light of its objectively grounded structure, that there emerged the explicit formulations of belief which were eventually to take the form of the early creeds (*Adv. haer.* 1.2, vol. I, pp. 90f; 3.1f, 4, vol. II, pp. 2ff; 25f; 4.1f, pp. 146ff; 4.53.1, pp. 261f; 5.20.1f, pp. 377f; *Epideixis*, 6). From the way in which Irenaeus handled these credal formulae, it would seem clear that they were not sets of doctrinal propositions logically deduced from the original Deposit of Faith but were coherent convictions in process of taking explicit form in the mind of the Church through a general consensus arising spontaneously out of the Apostolic Deposit of Faith and controlled by the implicit structure embodied in it. This incipient credal formulation of belief was not a 'hypothetical system' of ideas excogitated out of the inner religious consciousness of the Church and then arbitrarily and distortingly imposed upon the interpretation of the Gospel (*Adv. haer.* 1.18, vol. I, pp. 80ff; 2.40-5, pp. 347-58). Rather was it a disclosure of the internal unity and harmony of the Faith through a representation of the way in which different 'members of the Truth' are conjoined within the organic structure of 'the body of Truth'. The various beliefs are formulated in such a way that each is given its appropriate place within the coherent whole much like the limbs of a living body which cannot be severed from the body without dismemberment and destruction of the whole (*Adv. haer.* 1.15, vol. I, pp. 66f).

That is to say, the credal statements thus formulated by the Church cannot be abstracted from the objective substance of the whole coherent structure of the Faith, for they are what they are only through their conjoint embodiment in it. They are not statements which are connected with one another through some logico-deductive system, but statements which are ordered and integrated from beyond themselves by their common ground in the Apostolic Deposit of Faith and, in the final analysis, in the objective self-revelation of God in Jesus Christ. They are to be treated, therefore, not as complete but as incomplete statements, not as closed but as open formulations of belief, locked into Truth that exceeds their capacity adequately to express it. Although they fall short of what they intend, they are not for that reason false, since they do not have their truth in themselves but in that to which they refer independent of themselves, and are true in so far as they are 'rightly related' (*orthōs*) to it. Credal formulations of this kind that arise in the compulsive response to the objective self-revelation of God express sure and firm convictions for they are sustained beyond themselves, but on the other hand they have an open range which answers to the fact that even while God condescends to make himself known within the conditions of our human existence in space and time, as he has done in the Incarnation of his Word and Truth in Jesus Christ, nevertheless by his very nature he transcends the range of all our human knowledge and speech. That is to say, we have to reckon with the fact, as Irenaeus rightly insisted, that all theological knowledge and certainly all credal formulations of the Truth are only 'in part' (*ek merous*), for there is much that belongs only to God which we must frankly leave to him, for it would be impious even to think of intruding into it (*Adv. haer.* 2.15.3f, vol. I, pp. 282f; 2.41-3, pp. 349-58).

The incipient credal formulations which we find emerging in Irenaeus' theological interpretation of the Truth of the Gospel and his elucidation of the order implicit in the fundamental Deposit of Faith, already manifest the essential Trinitarian features of the Church's understanding of the Faith as it eventually came to explicit expression in the Nicene Creed. However, in the place and preponderance given to the

Christological formulae by Irenaeus, it is evident that it was at this point, in the indivisible union between God and Man in the Person of the Mediator and in the oneness of being and agency between the incarnate Son and the Father, that Irenaeus found the central connection in the inner structure of the Faith upon which faith in God the Father and in the Holy Spirit hinged, for in a significant sense they are presented as functions of faith in Jesus Christ the incarnate Word and Truth of God through whom and in whom we have access to the Father in one Spirit. That was clearly a feature that left its mark upon the developed organisation of the credal articles, although that was due, of course, not simply to Irenaeus but to the general consensus of the Church in the full unfolding of the Baptismal Creed particularly in the East into the Creed of Nicaea and Constantinople. So far as Irenaeus himself was concerned, however, all that was needed was an appropriate conception and form of speech to give the key-connection in the Mediator more adequate expression — and that is precisely what happened in the Council of Nicaea in the adoption of the expression *homoousios tō patri*.

With its adoption and insertion into the heart of the Creed at Nicaea, *homoousios* came to be used as a theological instrument to make clear the fundamental sense of the Holy Scriptures in their many statements about the relation of Christ the incarnate Son to God the Father, and to give expression to the ontological substructure upon which the meaning of these biblical statements rested and through which they were integrated in the Deposit of Faith. Thus the *homoousion* was of immense help to the Church in reaching clear and coherent belief in Jesus Christ as the incarnate Son of God and in providing the Church with a careful form of thought expressing the oneness in being between Christ and God as the all-important hinge between the statements of the Creed about God the Father, the Son and the Holy Spirit, as well as the statements about creation, salvation and final destiny. As such, however, far from being an explicit definition, *homoousios tō patri* in the context of the Nicene declaration of faith was essentially an exegetical and clarificatory expression to be understood under the control of the objective relation in God which it was forged to signify.

Nevertheless, once the *homoousion* became employed by the

Church in this way to bring to light the decisive relation between the incarnate Son and the Father, with which the very core of the Gospel and its ultimate validity were discerned to be bound up, it took on the role of an interpretative instrument of thought through which the Church's general understanding of the Evangelical and Apostolic Deposit of Faith was given more exact guidance in its mission to guard, defend, and transmit the Faith in its essential truth and integrity. The enshrining of the *homoousion* in the organic structure of the Nicene Creed, thereby bringing into sharp relief the inherent structure of the Gospel or Deposit of Faith, had the effect of making the Nicene Creed the operative canon of truth with reference to which the Church could continue to instruct the faithful, protect the Gospel from heretical distortion, and provide further doctrinal formulations as they might be needed.

It is highly significant that the Nicene Creed, even in the full form given to it by the Council of Constantinople in 381 A.D. retained the original character of the Deposit of Faith as embodied truth or embodied doctrine identical in the last analysis with the whole evangelical substance of Jesus Christ and his Gospel. At the same time, it brought to fruition the disclosure of the internal structure and harmony of the whole Deposit of Faith with which Irenaeus and others were so deeply engaged in the second and third centuries. That is to say, the Nicene-Constantinopolitan Creed was essentially a kerygmatic and charismatic declaration of the Faith once for all delivered to the saints with a deepened understanding of its objective Christocentric yet Trinitarian ground, but without any abstraction of its inherent conceptual organisation from that ground. The affirmations of belief hymned or proclaimed in the Creed, far from having the character of analytical doctrinal statements, were ways in which the coherent body of informal truth embedded in the foundation of the Church in Christ and his Gospel came to formal expression as it pressed upon the mind of the Church in its worship of God and in the fulfilment of its mission to mankind. It is because the Nicene Creed remained integrated with the embodied form of truth and doctrine in the original Deposit of Faith in this unique way, that it shared in its once for all character and status in the foundation of the Church, so that as such it constituted the controlling base with reference to which all other Conciliar Formulations of Christian doctrine were made.

This is not to claim that the Church in any Council ever put the Nicene Creed on the same level as the Faith once delivered to the saints in the definitive form given to it in the self-proclamation and self-interpretation of the Lord himself mediated through the Apostolic 'ministry of the Word' (Acts 6.4) under the inspiration of the Holy Spirit and deposited in the unrepeatable Apostolic Foundation of the Church. In that form the apostolic *kērygma* of the Gospel, received by direct revelation from Jesus Christ and handed on as the Deposit of Faith, was accorded a unique and authoritative place in the continuing life and faith of the Church. As such it was given decisive recognition in the formation of the canon of Holy Scripture, which had the effect of differentiating Apostolic Tradition sharply from all other tradition, and subordinating the whole stream of tradition in the Church to the Holy Scriptures in which the Apostolic Tradition had taken objective canonical and communicable form.

It is significant that it was in the process of this differentiation in the second century that the Deposit of Faith also took faint shape through there being brought to light the inherent structure which it embodied. The determination of the canon of Holy Scripture took a long time, but it took place by allowing those Scriptures which imposed themselves on the mind of the Church on the ground of their self-evidencing, authoritative mediation of divine revelation, and in virtue of their tested apostolicity in conveying the original *kērygma* of the Gospel, to be differentiated from other scriptures. Throughout the course of this elucidation there was constant interplay between the canon of truth and the canon of Holy Scripture. Only those Scriptures were accepted as mediating divine revelation which were in accord with the canon of truth in the Apostolic Deposit of Faith, and that tradition of faith was accepted as authentically Apostolic which was in accord with the teaching of the accepted Scriptures. In that process, however, the primacy accorded to the Apostolic Tradition over all other tradition carried with it the primacy of the Apostolic Scriptures. But the full formal acknowledgment of the Holy Scriptures took place only as the inner structure and harmony of the Holy Scriptures was found to be essentially the same as the inner structure and harmony found to be embodied in the Deposit of Faith.

That is precisely what we find emerging at the Council of Nicaea. On the one hand it was concerned with the faithful distillation of the fundamental sense of the Holy Scripture in its many statements about the relation of Christ to the Father through penetrating into the inner substance of the Gospel; but on the other hand it was concerned with giving clear explicit formulation to coherent belief in Jesus Christ the incarnate Son of God by bringing to light the nature of his relation to God the Father, and in so doing came up with the all-important *homoousios tō patri*. In doing that, however, it brought to decisive expression the ontological substructure upon which the meaning of the New Testament message about Jesus Christ rested and through which its different writings and statements concerning Christ and the Gospel could be integrated in accordance with their essential import. Thus by determining the inner structure of the Gospel through subordinating its mind to the teaching of the Holy Scriptures and the Apostolic mind that they enshrined, and giving that structure expression in the Creed, the Nicene Council had the effect of establishing in a hitherto unprecedented way the primacy of the Holy Scriptures in the mind of the Church. Certainly the Gospels and the Pauline Epistles had been accepted informally along with the Old Testament as of canonical authority by about the beginning of the third century, but it was only after the Nicene Council that the exact determination of the Canon was made. The integration of the basic convictions on which the Church had always relied in its worship and mission into a coherent pattern gave sharpness and precision to the Church's interpretation of the New Testament Gospel. But once that pattern had been discerned, and was found to underly the whole Apostolic presentation of the Gospel, something quite *irreversible* took place within the mind of the Church which could not be forgotten, for it gave expression to the theological framework which the Gospel of the incarnate, crucified and risen Son of God had created for itself in the understanding of the Church, and through which the Gospel was allowed to assert its own inherent force in shaping and regulating the teaching of the Church. It is hardly surprising, then, that the universal Church has ever since looked back upon the Nicene Council and the Nicene Creed with such awe and respect.

Several points may now be made in concluding this discussion of the Deposit of Faith.

(a) As we have seen, the Deposit of Faith is to be understood as spanning two levels. At the deepest level it is identical with the whole saving Event of the incarnate, crucified, and risen Son of God, but on another level it is identical with the faithful reception and interpretation of the Gospel as it took authoritative shape in the Apostolic Foundation of the Church and thus in the New Testament Scriptures. From the beginning these two levels were inseparably coordinated in the Deposit of the Faith, the second being governed and structured through the revelatory import and impact of the first upon it, so that it was made to point away from itself to Christ, who is the Truth in his own personal Being. In the Deposit of Faith, and in all interpretation of the Holy Scriptures, therefore, Jesus Christ himself, the *Ego Eimi* of the Truth of God, is the ultimate criterion to which everything is to be referred. He, the Truth himself, is the ultimate Judge of what is true or false in our understanding and interpretation of the Gospel and in our formulation of the truths and doctrines of the Faith. It was in that sense that Irenaeus spoke of the *canon of truth* (*kanōn tēs alētheias*) for the canon of truth is properly the truth itself in its own self-evidencing authority (*Adv. haer.* 2.4.1, vol. I, p. 349) and only in a secondary sense the regulative formulation of the truth. Although he does not seem to have used the expression *Autoalētheia*, which derives from the Alexandrian theologians, that is precisely what Irenaeus really meant by the canon of truth. But used in this sense the canon of truth refers to the Truth embodied in Christ and embodied by Christ through his own self-proclamation and self-interpretation in the Apostolic Foundation of the Church. It is *embodied truth*, not detached or abstract truth, with which the Nicene Creed is concerned.

(b) Now while the Nicene Creed represented an unfolding of the theological structure that informed the Deposit of Faith in the two-levelled way which we have noted, it was always possible for the central points distilled out of the interpretation of the Gospel, or crystallised out of the Deposit of Faith, to be detached from their embodiment in the foundation and life of the Church in Christ and organised into a system of truths on their own. A threat in that direction early appeared in the history of the Church, owing to the disruptive effects of underlying dualist modes of thought current in the ancient world. That seems to be what we find in the writings of Tertullian, who consistently regarded the rule of faith (*regula fidei*) as a fixed formula of truth for belief, which he claimed had been instituted by Christ himself and had been handed down entire and unchanged from the Apostles (*De praescr. haer.* 13, 20-28, 31-32). It represented what he called an 'irreformable' set of revealed doctrines which constituted 'the sum and substance' of all that is learned of God (*De prasecr.* 13; *Adv. Prax.* 2; *De virg. vel.* 1; *De anima*, 2). In accordance with his conception of the Gospel as a 'new law' (*nova lex*) inaugurated by Christ, Tertullian spoke of 'the faith deposited in the rule' as constituting a 'law' (*lex*) which must be observed as a condition of salvation (*De praescr.* 14). The rule of faith was the 'constant law of faith', which must be 'kept inviolate as a prescriptive rule' (*De virg. vel.* 1; *Adv. Prax.* 2), and was identified with the baptismal confession which he also described as 'the law of faith' (*De spect.* 4). That is to say, the *regula fidei* or *regula veritatis* was here turned into a legalistic principle. Something had clearly gone wrong with his understanding of the Deposit of Faith, for it tended to be restricted to a compendium of doctrines formulated in definitive statements which were regarded as themselves identical with the truths they were meant to express. Although he claimed that they had been handed down in this precise form, they were rather theological conceptions that had been abstractively derived from the original Deposit of Faith and formalised into a *system of doctrine* which must be imposed prescriptively upon the life and faith of the Church. The effect of this was to make the rule of faith no more and no less than a deposit of doctrinal propositions and indeed to make the very concept of the rule of faith itself into a doctrine.

(c) Fortunately the kind of outlook represented by Tertullian in his severely legalist approach to the Faith of the Church and his distinctly nominalistic conception of revealed truth in terms of doctrinal propositions, found little place in the Councils which gave us the Nicene-Constantinopolitan Creed. They retained the biblical conception of the wholeness of the Truth and the Faith, and found a way of expressing belief, not in analytical theological statements, but in a doxological de-claration of embodied truth and embodied doctrine. Thus in the Nicene Creed the Church was provided with a firm, inherently structured base, with constant reference to which it could go on to make further conciliar declarations and more explicit formulations of the truth of the Gospel, yet controlled by the paradigmatic way in which the Nicene and Constantinopolitan Fathers preserved and elucidated the heart and substance of the Gospel through consistent service to Holy Scripture and subjection of their own understanding to the *Autoalētheia* of divine Revelation.

(*d*) In the Western Church, however, the divergence represented by the views of Irenaeus and Tertullian, and a dualist, legalising movement of thought which tended to impose Tertullian-like ways of thinking upon the basic contributions of Irenaeus, have had very far-reaching effects. They have left their mark in various ways upon the Roman Catholic Church and the Evangelical Churches, not least in the lasting tension between tradition and Scripture and between what came to be called 'the substance of the Faith' and dogmatic formulations of the Faith. So far as the Roman. Church was concerned the ultimate identity of the Deposit of Faith and the Saving Event of Christ clothed with his Gospel tended to fall into the background, which had the effect of an unbalanced stress upon the embodiment of the Faith in the Church as such, annulling the early Patristic distinction between the Apostolic Tradition and ecclesiastical tradition. Moreover a bifurcation in the concept of the Deposit of Faith set in. On the one hand, the Faith was regarded as transmitted through its informal embodiment in the continuing life, faith and worship of the Church, and on the other hand, it was held to be transmitted through explicit dogmatic formulation of its conceptual content in a corpus of dogmatic truth under the guardianship of the teaching office of the Church. This bifurcation was not unrelated to the tension that developed out of the Middle Ages between the Church as mystical body and the Church as juridical institution or society. In reaction to the Reformation and its charges that the Roman Catholic Church kept on producing new dogmas which had no substance in the Apostolic Foundation of the Church, thus calling in question the concept of *una fides semper eadem*, and the basic principle of the Vincentian canon, *quod ubique, quod semper, quod ab omnibus creditum est*, the Roman Catholic Church came to lay increasing stress upon a distinction between *traditio passiva* and *traditio activa*, the former referring to the unchanging treasury of the Faith handed down through the ages, but the latter referring to the way in which the Church with the aid of the Holy Spirit takes out of the treasury of the Faith new truth as well as old truth. Also, in reaction to the Reformation emphasis upon *sola Scriptura* and its identification of Apostolicity with conformity to the New Testament Revelation, the Roman Catholic Church tended to stress more and more the infallible role of the Papacy as the supreme Teaching Office of the Church, and the irreformable nature of officially proclaimed dogmatic pronouncements. While this development came to a head in the First Vatican Council when dogmatic propositions about the truth were identified with the truth itself, a movement in the opposite direction has taken place in the Second Vatican Council, in which the Faith once delivered to the saints is identified once more with the Saving Event of Christ himself, with a central place being accorded to the Holy Scripture, and a distinction is drawn between the Deposit or Substance of Faith and dogmatic formulations about the Faith (*De divina revelatione*, II.10-III.12; *De ecclesia*, II.12; III.25; *Apostolicae Sedis*, 1962, 54, p. 792).

(*e*) The Evangelical Churches were admittedly caught up in the problems arising out of the deep tensions latent in the Western Church as a whole. The Reformation, however, stands for the fact that attempts were made to restore 'the Face of Christ in the Church' and thus to restore 'the face of the ancient Catholic Church'. That is to say, the Evangelical Churches brought back into the centre of their faith the emphasis upon the whole revealing and saving Event of Christ as constituting the very substance of the Gospel. And it was from that controlling centre that they assessed the historical transmission of the Faith in the life and mission of the Church, for they had to subject it to the primacy of the Apostolic Witness and Teaching embodied in the Holy Scriptures.

If John Calvin's thought may be taken to represent the central position taken in this respect by the Churches of the

Reformation, several things may be said. According to him, 'our whole salvation in all its parts is comprehended in Christ' (*Inst.* 2.26.29), and it is significant that his Christology in the second book of the *Institute* was largely governed by the Irenaean doctrine of the Incarnation. In Christ himself the whole treasury of divine knowledge and wisdom is hidden, and all that God has promised and fulfilled for our salvation is embodied in him, so that Christ himself is the proper object and substance of our faith (*Inst.* 2.9, 2-3, 13-15, 41, etc). By Christ, then, is meant not some bare Christ (*Christus nudus*) but Christ as he is given us by the Father and 'clothed with his own Gospel' (*evangelio suo vestitum*, *Inst.* 3.2.6). Expressions of this kind, 'Christ clothed with his promises', or 'Christ clothed with his benefits', were constantly repeated by Calvin to drive home the point that Christ cannot be separated from his saving Words and Acts; for they are for ever embodied in what he was and is. Christ gives himself to us wrapped up in his Word, for he dwells in the very Gospel he proclaims. This means that even now we can have access to Christ in 'the Word of the Truth of the Gospel' (Col. 1.5). It was this approach to Christ in the Reformation which lay behind its immense stress upon the sole Mediatorship of Christ and the living objective nature of the Word of God.

This understanding of Christ and the Gospel inevitably reinforced the Reformation emphasis upon the all-important place to be given to Holy Scripture and its supremacy over all tradition, for it is in the Holy Scripture, as Calvin expressed it, that God continues to bear living witness to himself and speaks to us personally, as if we hear his living voice (*Inst.* 1.6.2; 7.1,4). This does not mean that faith in God or the knowledge of God rests upon the Scriptures themselves, but rather upon the Truth of God himself, for the Scriptures are rather like spectacles which enable us to see things clearly beyond themselves (*Inst.* 1.6.1f; 7.1-2, 4-5; 8.1f). It is in this connection that Calvin refers to the *regula fidei*, yet not in the sense of Tertullian but of Irenaeus, in his account of the canon of truth or the *regula veritatis*, in which the Truth itself must be allowed to be the judge of the truth or falsity of our interpretation of Holy Scripture and our formulations of doctrine. It is not enough, he held, simply to appeal to Holy Scripture, since the interpretations invariably differ. We must test the fidelity of biblical interpretation or doctrinal formulation by tracing biblical statements back to the *Veritas Dei* to which they refer independent of themselves, and allow that Truth to retain the authority of its own divine Majesty without trying to bring it under our control (*Inst.* 1536, *Epist. ad Franciscum 1, Calvini Opera Selecta*, I, p. 23f; cf. also *Inst.* 1.7.3f; 8.1ff). While Calvin brought this into connection with what he called the *testimonium internum Spiritus Sancti* which enables us to read and hear the Word and Truth of God himself in the Scriptures, he insisted in line with his concept of the self-witness of God to us (*Inst.* 1.7.4f) that 'the Spirit inheres in the Truth of God' and as such brings the Majesty and Weight of that Truth to bear compellingly and convincingly upon us (*Inst.* 1.7.4; 8.1-2, 11, 13; 9.1-3). The appeal is then to the objective self-evidencing Reality of God's own eternal Truth, but that may be known only in accordance with what it is independently in itself and as we on our part submit our understanding to its authority and judgment as they bear upon us through the witness of Holy Scripture. In other words, here we have a return to the Patristic concept of *Autoalētheia* linked up with the Spirit of Truth.

In the general development of the Evangelical Churches, however, there has been a failure to appreciate adequately the living embodiment of faith and truth in the corporate life and structure of the Church. It is to be admitted that tensions have developed between Scripture and Confession, or biblicism and confessionalism, in which we find a Tertullian type of approach adopted both toward the Scripture and toward credal formulations of Christian doctrine. This is very evident in the way in which the *Canons of the Synod of Dort* or the *Westminister Confession of Faith* have had the effect of reducing the church's Confession of the Faith to systems of doctrinal propositions which are invested with prescriptive authority. On the other hand, it is very evident that these dualist and legalist approaches to the Faith are being undermined by a better understanding of the relation of *kērygma* to *dogma* and by the steady insistence that we must learn to distinguish the Substance of the Faith from explicit doctrinal formulations. Thus here again we have a return to the perspective of Nicene theology.

Autoexousia in the Life of the Church

With us human beings authority is not something that functions by itself but depends on something else that gives it its impelling force and something else again through which it is implemented; but this is not the case with God in whom will and action and the power of his divine Being perfectly coincide. This was the point recognised by the Alexandrian theologians when they spoke of God's Authority as *Autoexousia* in the same way in which they spoke of his Truth as *Autoaletheia*. *Aletheia* and *Exousia* are one in the *Ego Eimi* of his very Being as God, so that *Autoaletheia* and *Autoexousia* represent cognate ways in which we have to do with the ultimate Reality and Majesty of God himself. This applies also to God incarnate in Jesus Christ, for while in us will, word and act fall apart, for they are other than what we are in our personal beings, in him they remain one and undivided in the self-sufficiency and power of his Personal Being. Thus he is the *Autoexousia* as well as the *Autoaletheia* of God embodied in himself — that is to say, in Jesus Christ the ultimate *Exousia* of God exerts its inherent force in the incarnate *Ego Eimi* of his living presence with us in this world (Matt. 28:18-20). With him the Authority of his Word is identical with the Authority of his Act, and the Authority of his Act is identical with the Authority of his Person.

The Evangelists recount that the direct presence of that ultimate *Exousia* of God in Jesus created such astonishment and upheaval, that they regularly used words describing an earthquake to indicate its impact — people were aware that they were face to face with the *Eschaton*, the Judge of all the earth before whose Face nothing could be concealed, for even the innermost recesses of the human heart unknown to itself were laid bare before him. The Authority which people encountered in Jesus was utterly strange and new, unlike any other authority (Mark 1: 22, 27, etc.). He was man like any other man, physically conditioned in space and time, in whom willing, speaking and doing are different, whose words are in addition to his person and whose works are in addition to his words, but in Jesus the unity in God between Person, Word and Act had been made to overlap and gather in its embrace the differences between person, word and act in the creature, so that they were made to mediate God's Word, Act and Person to human beings through a oneness between Jesus Christ and God. Expressed in another way, in the hypostatic union between God and Man in Jesus Christ there was included a union between the Word of God and the word of man, the Act of God and the act of man, the Will of God and the will of man, in one Person, in such a way that the *Exousia* of God the Father Almighty assumed form within the creaturely and human conditions of space and time. That was the utterly unique nature of the *Exousia* of Jesus, which was quite unlike the *exousia* of the Scribes and Pharisees, but it was an *Exousia* which in its incarnate reality set all authority in space and time upon a new basis, thereby calling in question all the vaunted authorities, religious as well as secular, in this world.

Since God alone is the ultimate source of all authority and there are authorities in this world, we are accustomed to distinguish between primary and secondary authority, the absolute Authority of God and relative authority, the Lordly Authority of God and the subordinate authorities found everywhere in our human and social existence. The very nature of secondary authority is that it is relative and indirect, subject to the ultimate, direct Authority of God which it is meant to serve by letting Ultimate Authority have its proper place in all we think and say and do and are. But when secondary authorities stand in the way of Ultimate Authority, thereby usurping its place, they clothe themselves in its 'absoluteness' and inevitably become tyrannical and oppressive; that is, they become what the Scriptures speak of as demonic authorities, 'the authorities of darkness'. That was clearly the kind of authority that the direct presence of divine *Exousia* in Jesus Christ called in question, for his presence had the effect of showing that demonic authorities of this kind could become entrenched even in divinely appointed or sanctioned authorities, in legal and constitutional institutions, and in the Church as well as the State, and therefore of unmasking them with the seismic results which we have already noted. This critical effect upon established authorities, however, emanated from a positive base, the new kind of authority that emerged in space and time with the economic condescension of God's own

Autoexousia in the humiliation, weakness and meekness of Jesus — so that it is strictly from Jesus that we must take our guidance in understanding its nature and mode of operation.

The general perspective, of course must be Trinitarian, from the Father, through the Son and in the Spirit, but our controlling concept must surely be the self-operation of God's *Autoexousia* in the form of personal being in Jesus, the incarnate Son of God. Athanasius taught us that in the Incarnation God did not simply come *into man*, but without any diminishment of his full divine Reality came *as man* (*Con. Arianos*, 3.30, 38, 47; *Ad Epictetum*, 2, etc.). Similarly we must think that in the Incarnation the *Exousia* of God did not just come into man and operate in him, in Jesus, but came *as Man, as Jesus*, and thus operated in a human way, *anthropinōs*, i.e., not by naked divine fiat but in a lowly way identical with the actual way taken by Jesus for us and our salvation from his birth of the Virgin Mary to his Crucifixion and Resurrection. As in Jesus we have the acute personalisation of all God's ways and works with mankind, so in Jesus we must think of the *Autoexousia* of God incarnate operating in an intensely personal and personalising way, that is, never by impersonal command or detached deed, but always and only in such a way that he is immediately and personally present in his word and act with the undiminished *Ego Eimi* of his divine-human Being. While we creaturely human beings are persons only in inter-relation with other creaturely persons, nevertheless we are created persons with no self-subsistence of our own. We draw the very substance of our personal being from the Triune God who in the fulness of his Personal Being is the one Source of all personal being. Each of us is *persona personata*, but Jesus Christ the Son of God incarnate, is *Persona personans*. Embodied in this Jesus Christ the divine *Autoexousia* is the self-operating Person-Authority which functions not only in a personal, but in a person-constituting way, that is, by way of communion or *koinōnia* as its corporate coefficient in the life and mission of the Church.

In the nature of the case the actualisation and exercise of this unique divine *Exousia* within the conditions of our estranged and sinful humanity had to take on an essentially *redemptive form*. That became clear right away in the temptations of Jesus immediately after his baptismal consecration as the Lamb of

God to bear away the sin of the world, when he entirely renounced any reliance upon or appeal to demonstrative force or worldly power and chose instead the humble way of 'the Servant' and the way of the Cross. Historically speaking, it was because Jesus rejected the role of a political messiah and the kind of in-built violence which it involved that he was crucified by the 'authorities' of Church and State, as he made very clear in the parable he told during his passion week in answer to the question 'By what *exousia* do you do these things?' He had taken the way of incarnational penetration into the depths of our alienated human being in order to get at the root of evil and the irreversibility of guilt entrenched there and thus deal decisively with them through expiatory sacrifice and atoning mediation. That is why the New Testament points to the Cross as the place where the saving Will and redemptive Activity of God were focused, the place where God's *Exousia* was triumphant over all the powers and authorities of this world (Col. 1.13ff). It was only by coming under the power-structures of this world and penetrating into their foundations that he was able to break their strangle-hold upon us, or, to use Pauline language, it was only as he was made under the law that he redeemed those who were under the law, making it possible for them to become sons of God (Gal. 3 & 4; Romans 3 & 6). Within the estranged and twisted relations between man and God the very law given by God to serve his supreme Authority had been inverted on itself as though it had an authority of its own, so that it became 'the strength of sin' and exercised a cursed tyranny over the guilty human conscience (Gal. 3.9ff). But God dealt so decisively with this state of affairs through atonement that he set the law upon a new basis, and to all who believed in the incarnate Son he brought freedom to become sons of God through sharing *exousia* with them (John 1:12).

Here we learn that the distinctive feature of the *Autoexousia* of God in its actualisation and exercise through the saving economy of Jesus Christ is that it operates not through sheer power as the world understands it but through the weakness of the Man on the Cross, for, as it is expressed in the Apocalypse, it was not as a mighty Lion but as a Lamb that the incarnate Son of God was able to break open the sealed book of guilt and destiny, and rule over all history (Rev. 5). Hence with the

Incarnation the *Exousia* of God takes on a redemptive pattern demanding a soteriological understanding of its nature and exercise. Thus the Gospel tells us that in the life and passion of Jesus Christ, 'the Servant of the Lord', we are provided with the *hypodeigma* of how we are to regard the actualisation and functioning of *exousia* (John 13:15). That is why Jesus warned his disciples at the Holy Supper, at the very point when he invested them with authority in his Kingdom, that they were not to model their notion or exercise of authority upon power-structures of the secular world (Luke 22: 24-30; cf. Mark 10:42f; Matt. 20:25f). Moreover, it was because of this intrinsically soteriological nature of the incarnate *Exousia* of God, that Jesus pointed explicitly to the ministry of forgiveness in his Name as the point of transmission of *exousia* from himself to his disciples (Matt. 18:18; John 20:23). That is why the regular sharing of divine *exousia* in the Church centres in and takes its structural pattern from the stewardship (*oikonomia*) in the mysteries of God in 'the word of the truth of the Gospel' and in the celebration of Baptism and Eucharist.

The passages from the Gospels we have just referred to point us to another all-important feature of the incarnate *Exousia*, namely, its actualisation within the community of the faithful gathered in the Name of Christ and in the Spirit, through whom Christ is immediately present in his *Ego Eimi* as the risen Lord. That is to say, in seeking to understand the actualisation and operation of *Autoexousia* we must take fully into account the movement *in the Spirit* as well as *through the Son*, although as our Lord made clear, as sent by the Father in the Name of the Son the Holy Spirit does not act 'from himself' (*aph' heautou*) but ministers what he receives from Christ (John 16:13f). The point that concerns us now is that *exousia* is exercised and transmitted in the Spirit by way of communion or *koinōnia*, in both senses of that term, through the participation of people in the Church in the Spirit and through their membership with one another in the Body Christ. That is to say, what we are concerned with here is the embodiment of the *Exousia* of Christ within the life and mission of the Church in such a way that through the communion of the One Spirit who dwells in Christ and in his Church uniting them internally to one another, it serves the living dynamic *Ego Eimi* of Christ in his own *Autoexousia*, the self-sufficient and self-sustaining *Exousia* of God incarnate in him. Thus the *exousia* embodied in the Church and ministry is not to be thought of as externally and indirectly related to Christ, in merely moral or juridical ways, but as internally and directly related to him through union and communion with him as he on another level is internally and directly related to the Father through the union and communion of the Holy Trinity.

Since the *Autoexousia* and *Autoalētheia* of Christ are not disparate but are modes of one and the same divine Reality, we must think of the embodiment of Christ's Authority in the corporate life and mission of the Church in much the same way as we thought of the embodiment of the Truth of Christ in the faith and life of the Church. We recall that the Deposit of Faith is to be understood as spanning two levels: the primary level where it is identical with the whole saving Event of Christ, Christ clothed with his Gospel of saving Words and Acts, and the secondary level where it is identical with the faithful reception and interpretation of Christ and his Gospel as it came to authoritative shape in the Apostolic Foundation of the Church, and thus in the canon of the New Testament Scriptures. While those two levels are inseparably coordinated in the Faith once delivered to the saints, the second is governed and structured through the inspired impact of the first upon it so that it is made to point away from itself to Christ. It is in the same way that we have to think of Christ clothed with his own *Exousia* in his unrepeatable Incarnation, and Christ livingly and dynamically present with his own *Exousia* in the Church which through the Apostles he grounded once for all upon himself. In the Faith of the Church we do not have to do with Christ apart from the truth of Christ or with the truth of Christ apart from Christ himself, but with the whole living Reality of Christ clothed with his Truth who continues in the power of the Spirit to function as the *Autoalētheia* in and through the Church's faithful pro-clamation of Christ and teaching of his truth. Likewise in the Mission of the Church we do not have to do with Christ apart from the authority of Christ or with the authority of Christ apart from Christ himself, but with the whole living Reality of Christ invested with his Authority who continues in the power of the Spirit to function as the *Autoexousia* in and through the faithful ministry of the Church in his Name. While the Truth that Christ is cannot be resolved into the truth of the Apostles' teaching about him, nevertheless the Apostolic interpretation of Christ clothed with his Truth is the one form through which people continue to have access to Christ, which helps to make the Apostolic Scriptures so uniquely authoritative for us. Likewise, while the Authority of Christ cannot be resolved into the authority of the Apostolic ministry of Christ, nevertheless the authority of the Apostolic ministry received from Christ is the one norm which continues to mediate to people the Authority of Christ, which helps to make the Apostolic ministry so uniquely authoritative for us. Quite clearly in the Apostolic foundation of the Church in which Christ embodied his self-revelation and his self-authority, the Apostolic Scriptures and the Apostolic ministry cannot be separated, for they were integrated together in their mediation of the authoritative Word and Truth of Christ, and thus constituted the structural base for the normative proclamation and teaching of the Gospel in the historical life and mission of the Church.

That is precisely how we find Irenaeus interpreting the Apostolic foundation of the Church, as the unique and once for all embodiment of the Truth and Authority of Christ which came to expression in the Scriptures and Ministry emanating from the Apostles and which together constituted the Apostolic Tradition of the Faith in a form that was always one and the same. We have already discussed his account of the sacred Deposit of Faith as the source of the Church's continual renewal in Christ and his Gospel, and of the way in which the Church's faithful defence of the Gospel had the effect of allowing the intrinsic trinitarian structure of the Faith to come to view in more explicit formulation, and of how that functioned as the canon of truth in the interpretation of the Scriptures and understanding of the Faith, namely, by letting the Truth that Christ himself is be the ultimate judge of the Church's understanding of it. But our concern now is with Irenaeus' realisation that knowledge of the Truth of the Gospel is not given or handed down from the Apostles in an abstract or detached form but in a concrete embodied form in the Church where it is to be grasped only within the normative pattern of the faith and the normative structure of the Church as they were integrated together in the Apostolic Foundation of the Church in Christ. Thus he insisted that true knowledge has to do not only with the teaching of the Apostles but with 'the ancient constitution of the Church' (*to archaion tēs ekklēsias systēma*) which is authenticated to us as having the imprint of the Body of Christ through the succession of bishops and the unity and identity of the Faith mediated through them (*Adv. haer.* 4.53.2, vol. II, p. 262; cf. 5.20.1, p. 378).

As Irenaeus understood it, the communion with God through Christ and in the Spirit, which arises out of the reconciling and healing assumption of estranged humanity in the Incarnation, necessarily took a corporate and structured form as the Body of Christ. To that Church God has entrusted the Deposit of Faith, upon it he has poured out his Holy Spirit, and in it he has provided his people with ordinances through which the Spirit operates. 'Where the Church is, there is the Spirit of God, and where the Spirit of God is, there is the Church and every grace: but the Spirit is Truth.' (*Adv. haer.* 3.38, vol. II, p. 132). While Irenaeus pointed to the Church as the location of 'well-grounded knowledge' of the Truth embodied in it, he nevertheless laid the emphasis upon the objective self-revelation of God through Christ and in the Spirit as the actual source of our knowledge of the Truth (*Adv. haer.* 3.38.1-2, pp. 131f; 4.53.1-2, pp. 261ff; 5.20.1, pp. 378f.). Significantly with reference to 1 Timothy 3:15, he did not speak of the Church itself as 'the pillar and ground of Truth', but of 'the Gospel and the Spirit of Life' as 'the pillar and ground of the Church' (*Adv. haer.* 3.11.11, p. 47). For Irenaeus the intrinsic pattern of the Faith embodied in the Church and the organic structure of the Church are inwardly connected through the union and communion of the Church with Christ as his Body, but only in such a way that the pattern of the Faith and the structure of the Church point beyond themselves to the level of the embodied Truth and Authority in Christ himself, which they are meant to serve. Thus care was taken not to allow the embodiment of truth and authority in the Church to usurp the primacy of Truth and Authority in Christ the one Head and only Lord of the Church. That is what fidelity to the Apostolic foundation of the Church in Christ finally meant, and it was that fidelity which the *diadochē presbyterōn* and the *diadochē episkopōn* were meant to guard.

Just as Irenaeus operated with a concept of embodied truth

and embodied doctrine in the Church, so he operated also with a concept of *embodied authority*, with a ministry with which Christ shared *exousia* in its proclamation of the Gospel and pastoral care of the people, to be exercised according to the *hypodeigma* of service exhibited by Jesus himself, but with the promise that he himself would be with the ministry so that their proclamation and teaching of the Word of the Gospel in his name would indeed be empowered as the saving Word of God, and whatever they loosed on earth would be loosed in heaven, and whatever they bound on earth would be bound in heaven. By its very nature this *embodied and shared exousia* was characterised by several very essential features which we must note.

(*a*) Authority emanating through the Spirit from Christ in whom the Person of the Saviour, the Word of Salvation and the Act of Salvation belonged inseparably together, was authority that could not be separated from embodied truth or embodied doctrine. Since authority and truth are one and the same in Christ, they must be one and the same at the level where Christ shares them with the members of his Body. While the life and mission of the Church are episcopally, presbyterally and diaconally ordered, this ministerial structure is grounded in and governed by the Word of the Truth of the Gospel embodied in the Church from its Apostolic foundation, and as such it must be rightly related (*orthōs*) to the Truth as it is in Jesus Christ and coordinated with the intrinsic structure of the truth as it has come to trinitarian expression in the Church's fundamental Confession of Faith, as at the Nicene Council. That is to say, the structure of the ministry is *de fide* in its basic character, and is authentically authoritative in so far as it is geared into and reflects the intrinsic structure of truth and doctrine embodied in the Church. That is why Irenaeus insisted that succession in ministry and succession in the truth are not to be separated from one another. However, because of this *de fide* character of the ministry in its structure and authority, it is constantly open to theological adjustment in accordance with the truth of the Gospel and the Church's deepening understanding of it.

(*b*) Authority of this embodied kind is not transmitted through external moral or judicial relations but only internally through union and communion with Christ, which means that authority in the Church is actualised and exercised in Christ only by way of *koinōnia*. It is thus very different from secular notions of delegated authority or externally sanctioned authority, and in fact conflicts with it in much the same way in which the *Exousia* of Christ conflicted with the *exousia* of the Scribes and Pharisees. The Authority of Christ was exercised only through his intrinsic oneness in Being and Agency with the Father, and never independently, as we learn so fully from the Fourth Gospel. Correspondingly, authority in the Church is actualised and exercised only through *koinōnia*, in the twofold movement of conjoint participation of the members of the Church in Christ and in their mutual sharing with one another in him. Within this *koinōnia* both the ministry and the authority in which it shares take on an essentially *corporate* form. Thus in Cyprian, for example, the episcopate is shown to have a basically corporate nature such that it can be held only *in solidum* in the mutual relations of all bishops grounded in and controlled from the one Episcopate of Christ himself. It was this corporate nature of the ministry and of authority which gave rise to the Councils of the Church in which bishops held and exercised their authority only in and through *koinōnia* in the double sense we have noted. This basically corporate concept of the ministry, however, does not argue for the isolation of bishops from presbyters and deacons or indeed from the general membership of the Church and the one Priesthood of Christ in which through the Spirit it participates. This is the ground for the emphasis in the Reformed Church upon the 'corporate episcopate' or 'presbytery' within which the bishop is president or *proestōs* but apart from which he is not properly bishop. Our concern here, however, is not with the ministry as such but with the nature of ministerial authority in the Church and the mode of its exercise in union and communion with Christ in the Spirit.

(*c*) The third feature we have to take into account is the transcendent Authority of the sheer *Holiness* of God. This was an aspect of the divine Majesty of which the Old Testament saints were so awesomely aware, as we find, for example, in the prophet's vision of 'the Lord high and lifted up' before whose presence the seraphim covered their faces — from which we derive the *Trisagion* (Isaiah 6.1ff). In the New Testament we find the same intimate relation between the *Exousia* embodied in Jesus and the presence of the absolute Holiness of God in him which brought awe to his disciples and put to flight the powers of darkness. However, it was with the Resurrection of Christ as Lord and the pouring out of his Holy Spirit at Pentecost that the Church became so profoundly aware of the sheer Authority of Holiness as the impact of the sublime Majesty of God upon them through Jesus and in his Spirit. Moreover the warning of our Lord that sin against the Holy Spirit would not be forgiven and the death of Annias and Sapphira who lied to the Holy Spirit made an immense impression upon the Early Church, for in and through the Spirit they had to do with the absolute Authority of divine Holiness, Majesty and Glory. It is surely in connection with the mediation of the Holiness of God Almighty through the Son and in the Spirit that we are to understand the stress upon *theōsis* in Patristic theology, in accordance with the Lord's will that we be 'perfect' as the Father is Perfect and holy as he is Holy. It is above all in the worship of God, Father, Son and Holy Spirit, that the Holiness of God bears immediately upon us, relating us inwardly to the *Autoexousia* of God in such a way that conscience (*syneidēsis*) arises and is quickened within us, that is, the *con-scientia* of the faithful in their conjoint awareness of God. It is through this mode of knowing together with God and with one another before the Face of his Holiness and Majesty and under the compelling Authority of his transcendent Truth that there emerges and takes shape within the mind of the faithful the general consensus which is the full corporate coefficient of the *Exousia* of Christ in his Body the Church. It is to this sanctified conscience that we must link the stress noted earlier upon *eusebeia* or *theosebeia* in the Church's knowledge and formulation of truth and doctrine, that is, the devout, godly and reverent recognition of God's self-revelation, and a correspondingly godly, worthy and holy way of thinking and speaking of him, and not least of worshipping him in the Holy Spirit. This is what it means for the Church to act only in the Name of the Father, Son and Holy Spirit, since it is in that Name that the authority of the whole Church and its ministry of the Gospel rests, and not in any sense in its own name or in the name of any of its ministers.

We must now ask what became of this concept of the *wholeness of exousia* as it was embodied in the Church indivisibly integrated with embodied truth and embodied doctrine in the Foundation of the Church laid by Christ once and for all in the Apostles.

That was clearly the concept of *exousia* that came to canonical expression in the Councils of Nicaea and Constantinople, to which all Christendom is irreversibly indebted. There can be no doubt that that original wholeness was disrupted in varying degrees by underlying dualist forms of thought and life. Even when the Church overcame them in its understanding of the Trinity and Christ, and allowed the inner relation in Being and Agency between the Son and the Spirit to govern its formulation of the Creed, in triumph over all Arian and semi-Arian positions, it fell short of overcoming and transforming the dualist structures deeply embedded in the social, legal and political institutions of the Graeco-Roman world, with the result that they corroded from below and distorted the functioning of authority in the Church. The internal relation of authority in the Church to the incarnate Authority of Christ tended to give way to an external, legal relation, while the transmission of authority through *koinōnia* tended to be replaced by the devolution of authority through socio-political institutions.

This change had the effect of laying the Church open to the temptation, to which it all too often succumbed, of borrowing many of its external ecclesiastical forms from the hierarchical structures in the Byzantine and Roman Courts which carried with them a very different kind of authority with very different ends in view. This is very evident from the way in which bishops came to be invested with the powers of magistrates and accorded a 'lordly' status in society in the East as well as the West, but it is nowhere more evident than in the concept and institution of Primacy in the Church as the concrete manifestation of the supreme Authority of Christ and the controlling centre of its devolution down the hierarchical structure. Along with all this, at least in the Western Church, is found a basically dualist doctrine of the Church after the analogy of the soul and the body, as a 'mystical body' and a 'juridical institution', together with the development from the time of Leo the Great of the *codex iuris canonici* which led to severely juridical concepts of ecclesiastical doctrines and ordinances. It was in this way that the biblical concept of 'the principate of Peter', was altered through schematising the idea of succession from Peter in the See of Rome to pre-Christian Roman property law about inheritance and succession. Most basic of all, perhaps, was the fundamental change in the very concept of authority which this involved, as the Western notion of *auctoritas*, which still retained a distinctly personal quality, was steadily replaced by that of *potestas* or *sacra potestas*, while the very concept of *potestas* was itself split between *potestas ordinis* and *potestas iurisdictionis*, the former being exercised only within the sphere of the latter. The wide prevalence of this dualist and legalist concept of authority in the Western Church is evident from the fact that even the Reformed Church became trapped within it, as one can see from the appeal to *potestas ordinis* and *potestas iurisdictionis* in the Second Book of Discipline of the Church of Scotland, although that is somewhat modified by the insistence that Church discipline takes place through the preaching and teaching of the Word of the Gospel, and that the authority of the Gospel functions in the Church through the corporate Episcopate or Presbytery. Of course the traditional office of 'the bishop' had become controversial owing to the investment of episcopal office in the Western Church with socio-political juridical status and power, together with the segregation of the bishop from the corporate authority of the whole Presbytery and the whole Church meeting in synodical Council. The Reformed Church made a serious attempt to recover the ancient Catholic notion of 'embodied authority', but does not show much evidence of a recovery of the ancient Catholic notion of 'embodied truth' or 'embodied doctrine'. This is rather surprising, since through John Calvin the Reformed Church reintroduced into theology the original biblical and patristic doctrine of the Church as the Body of Christ, in contrast to the Western Mediaeval dualist notion of the Church as a juridical body animated by the Spirit or suffused by divine 'grace' as its soul. Calvin's doctrine of the Church, to be sure, had some influence on the *Tridentine Catechism* I.x; but it was not to be officially reappropriated by the Roman Catholic Church until *Lumen Gentium*, the 'dogmatic constitution' on the Church promulgated by the Second Vatican Council, in which, incidentally, the canonical doctrine of the *potestas ordinis* and *potestas iurisdictionis* is reinterpreted in terms of *munera* after the pattern of the *triplex munus* of Christ which had also been reintroduced by Calvin from patristic theology!

CHAPTER 6

THE TRINITARIAN STRUCTURE OF THE CHURCH AND ITS AUTHORITY

EMILIANOS TIMIADIS

Holy Trinity: basic foundation of the Church

In the third century many neophytes wondered whether they really belonged to the promised Church of the new Israel. Origen's disciples of the Alexandrian School often asked their master how the prophecies of the OT about the chosen People of God could apply in their case. They had particularly in mind those texts of Zechariah with regard to the eschatological days following the captivity, when 'a Branch will grow who shall build the temple of the Lord; and he shall bear the glory, and he shall sit and rule upon his throne, and he shall be priest upon his throne: and the counsel of peace shall be between them both . . .' (6:9-15). What was the meaning of such a metaphor? Such promising messianic texts could easily be misunderstood and differently applied by the Jews in their own interest. Allegory and typology nevertheless were the key to their orthodox interpretation. Origen (c. 185-254), in his commentaries, does not hesitate to affirm that all these texts prefigure Christ and anticipate their fulfilment in his Church, edified through faith in a Trinitarian God:

> 'He who will confess the divinity of the Lord, will build the house of the Lord, that is, the Church of the living God. This is the divine *Logos*. But equally, according to other interpretations, those who are raised above, as subjects of the Universal King and disciples of the Good Master, having put into practice the commandments of him who rules and instructs them, these also have built their lives, as a house, on the rock which is Christ; they

have established the bases and foundations of the house on
faith, stable and indestructible, in the Trinity. This is the
very same rock designed and recognised by Christ himself:
"You are Peter and on this rock I shall build my Church,
and the gates of Hades will not prevail against her"' (Mt.
16:18). (Text from the papyrus of Toura: *Comment. in
Zachariam*, liv.ii, 60; SC 84, p. 456.)

A few centuries later Maximus the Confessor, a profound
Byzantine writer (580-662), expounds the structure, mission
and events in the life of the Church. His answer constitutes the
famous treatise, *Mystagogia*. Here he evokes in glowing terms the
mystery of this assembly of believers. For Maximus, the Church
carries out, and carries on, what the Triune God intends for his
creation, leading humanity on to its finality, oneness, reconciliation and perfect state. He admits that humanity is divided,
broken, fallen, alienated, uprooted from its very sources and
origins. But instead of having a pessimistic approach, giving up
all hope of improvement, his exposition is full of optimism and
conviction. He believes in man's restoration. Man can become
different, better; he can attain his original 'pre-fall' state. This is
precisely the main task of the Church on earth, fulfilling God's
plan for salvation.

The Church, for this healing and redeeming task, he states,
has God himself as her model: τῷ θεῷ ὡς ἀρχετύπῳ εἰκὼν
ἐνεργοῦσα. Its members may differ externally, being composed
of men, women and children, a variety of races and colours,
languages, cultures, social views, civilizations, manners,
customs, professions, ranks and intellectual attainments. And
yet, from this uneven, heterogeneous material, the Church is
mandated to re-form and gradually create a totally new
humanity. She is commissioned to offer equally to all a divine
form and right of appeal, stemming from Christ and bearing his
name: Μίαν πᾶσι κατὰ τὸ ἴσον δίδωσι καὶ χαρίζεται θείαν μορφὴν
καὶ προσηγορίαν, τὸ ἀπὸ Χριστοῦ καὶ εἶναι καὶ ὀνομάζεσθαι. He
adds that this saving action is carried out by the Holy Trinity
through the Church, in order that each one may become God-
like. His language is obviously taken from Denys the Areopagite
(*Mystagogia* I, 1-2; P.G. 91, 665-669).

It is noteworthy that today a new awareness of the

Trinitarian basis of the Church is emerging. Vatican II has led
to self-criticism and questioning as to the practical consequences
of the present action of the Trinity as compared with the past.
Disapproval of a vaguely deistic spirituality is evident; so is a
greater emphasis on the action of the Church in history through
the action of the Holy Spirit (Marie-Dominique Chenu: 'The
new awareness of the Trinitarian basis of the Church', *Concilium*
146, June 1981, pp. 14-21).

In Jesus Christ humanity has been called to communion with
God the Father and the Holy Spirit. In him the eternal Will of
the Triune God has been revealed. The mystery of the Church is
linked to this Will in an inner and essential way. As the mystery
of the Triune God is experienced in its *energeia*, so is the mystery
of the Church, because the Church as a divine institution is
equipped with 'the same *energeia* as God, though in the guise of
imitation and image' (ὡς τὴν αὐτὴν αὐτῷ κατὰ μίμησιν καὶ τύπον
ἐνέργειαν ἔχουσαν), as Maximus the Confessor writes in
Mystagogia I, 1. The unity and the life of those who believe in the
Triune God reflect the fullness of the unity and the life of the
three persons of the Holy Trinity himself and have their source
in them (Jn. 14-17).

In listening to the proclaimed Word, the ensuing answer of
faith and the incorporation through Baptism in the name of the
Triune God, the life of the believer begins. It grows and is
sustained through the sacramental life. It is a gift of the Father
through Jesus Christ in the Holy Spirit. Christ's continuing
presence in the Church unto the ends of the earth (Mt. 28:20)
and the activity of the Holy Spirit within the Church transform
human beings and indeed the whole creation (Rom. 8:19-22)
into a *kainē ktisis* (2 Cor. 5:17; Rom. 12:2). This is the earthly
pledge of the eschatological consummation of humanity, the
future fulfilment of the reign of God; the Father through his Son
and the Holy Spirit conveys his essential and uncreated grace
and glory to creation.

Through the Incarnation, Cross, Resurrection and Ascension
of Christ, and through the mission, the coming and the
remaining of the Holy Spirit, the Church is a divine-human
foundation; in it the believers are members of the one Body of
Christ; Christ, as Head of the Body, is the Lord, the source of life
and the goal of the Church (Eph. 1:22; 4:15). The believers

participate in the fulness of the life of Christ, experienced by receiving his body and blood. Through his Church Christ leads humanity and the cosmos to unity under the Triune God (Eph. 1:10, 23).

Because of this existing essential relationship of the Triune God to his Church, the Trinitarian confession is fundamental to the identity of the Church, to the appropriate response of the one Faith; it is the indispensable sign of the unity of all believers. Thus, in the pre-Anaphora section of the Divine Liturgy, to the admonition of the celebrant: 'Let us love one another, that with one mind we may confess', the people proclaim their faith in the Holy Trinity: 'Father, Sonand Holy Spirit, the Trinity one in essence and undivided', followed by the recitation of the Creed.

Trinitarian interaction

An approach to the question of trinitarian doctrine cannot, therefore, ignore the interaction of the Triune God in the life of the Church. Triadology and ecclesiology are interrelated. From the earliest times only those baptized in the name of the Triune God were accounted as members of the Church and lived out all the dimensions of liturgical life. For them, life in Christ was identical to life in the Church, fully united to it and not on its periphery. This was for them the richest experience, where real communion in Christ was developed and the sustenance of their new life was assured. We have to remember that, while they were so attached to faith in an unique God, throughout their ministry the Apostles were activated by the conviction that there existed, above all, a Triune interaction. It was during the Eucharist that the Trinitarian action was proclaimed and the Confession of the Triune God solemnly sung by the assembly.

Christ often refers to his Father, proclaiming that God is also our God and our Father. He refers at the same time to the Paraclete: 'But when the Counsellor comes, whom I shall send to you from the Father, even the Spirit of truth, who proceeds from the Father, he will witness to me' (Jn. 15:26). This first experience of the life in Jesus has enabled us to see the ties in him, as yet beyond description — but ties of which, from now on, believers cannot but take advantage.

After the Resurrection and Pentecost, when the first

Christians began to live as disciples of Christ in an ecclesial fellowship, they had another experience: that of staying 'united in Jesus'. Modelling themselves on the Trinitarian love, like Jesus they prayed to the Father and were guided by the Spirit. Full of awe and reverence, they still avoided any formulation of the Trinity. Setting aside all scrupulous investigation, they lived, as one can now say, according to the following principle: only one God, but three Persons, three relations (σχέσεις). These relations were of love and equal honour (ἰσοτιμία). Jesus had shown in the parable of the Prodigal Son to what extent the Father was loving. Jesus Himself was nothing other than Love, and he asked for nothing else than love: 'Love the Father, love me, and love each other as I have loved you'. One could see effectively that the Spirit was a source of love, a source of communion and sanctification.

Gregory of Nyssa relates this love from the Father to the Son, by referring to a parallelism recorded in St. John's Gospel: 'That the love wherewith thou hast loved me may be in them, and I in them' (Jn. 17:26).

> 'If the Father loves the Son, and since we all believing on the Son become his Body, consequently, he who loves his own Son, loves also his Son's Body as the Son. We constitute the Body' (*Oratio* in I Cor. xv, 28; *PG* 44, 1321).

Out of this sprang the great revelation that God has love for us because he is love himself. We witness a Trinitarian relationship based on the mutual love of each Person, where the difference is only apparent, necessary to communion. Each time we speak of the Trinity, we must think of nothing else but love. Pentecost is a celebration of the love of God. God is Love and the Church is the outpouring of love, of a Trinitarian Philanthropia. In the last prayer of Jesus before his crucifixion, he asked for only one thing, unbelievable and striking for all of us: 'Father, I pray that the love you have shown to me, may be in them' (Jn. 17:21). The mission of the Church, therefore, ensues from its nature as the Body of Christ, sharing in the ministry of Christ as Mediator between God and his Creation. This mediation of Christ involves two integrally related movements: one from the Triune God to the creation, and the other from the creation to God. The Church manifests God's love for humanity in a Christian identification with all the creation, in a parallel *kenōsis*, in loving service and joyful proclamation.

This faith in God's Spirit, reconciling and uniting, is seen throughout the whole of ecclesiastical and secular history. In spite of errors — heresies — the Spirit keeps the Church One, working out her renewal and sanctification, leading her to perfect union with her Bridegroom. Both the Spirit and the Bride say to the Bridegroom, Jesus: 'Come!' (Rev. 22:17). Thus for Cyprian of Carthage, the universal Church appears as 'one assembled people in the unity of the Father, Son and Holy Spirit' (*De Orat. Domin.* 23; *PL* 4, 553). For him, membership of the Church is a common response to the call to holiness — the holiness of God himself:

> 'The spouse of Christ cannot be defiled; she is incorrupt
> and chaste. One home she knows: the sanctity of one
> chamber she guards with modesty and purity. It is she
> who keeps us for God, it is she who appoints unto the
> Kingdom the sons she has borne. Whoever, separating
> himself from the Church, is joined to an adulteress, is cut
> off from the promises of the Church; nor will he who
> leaves the Church of Christ attain to Christ's promises'
> (*De unitate Ecclesiae*, VI).

Today, too, the Church, in that same identification with all humanity, lifts up to God its pain and suffering, hope and aspirations, joy and thanksgiving in intercessory prayer and eucharistic worship. Any imbalance between these two directions of the mediatory movement adversely affects our ministry and mission to the world.

Only a Church fully aware of how people in the world live, feel and think can adequately fulfil both aspects of this mediatory mission. It is at this point that the Church recognises the validity and significance of different ministries, so that it may better understand and be in closer solidarity with the world, knowing and sharing its pain and yearning. For only by responding attentively to others can we abolish our own ignorance and misunderstanding of them, and so be better able to minister to them.

The fullness of our life has not as components this or that

human success or possession. There is another area waiting to be filled and taken care of. This is the Trinitarian relationship within our personal life. To this, Cyril of Jerusalem draws attention in talking to the catechumens before him:

'The only really true life is the Father, the source of gifts from above to all beings through the Son in the Holy Spirit'
('Η ὄντως ζωὴ καὶ ἀληθῶς ἔστιν ὁ Πατήρ ὁ δι' Υἱοῦ τοῖς ἅπασιν, ἐν ἁγίῳ Πνεύματι, τὰς ἐπουρανίους πηγάζων δωρεάς)
(*Catechesis* XVIII, 29; P.G. 33, 1049).

In this earthly situation, human beings seek something beyond the relative, temporal and corruptible. They are insecure and dissatisfied, and feel the limits of every pleasure. They turn to their innermost feelings, but without finding what is expected. They seek the real life, a life which cannot be produced by similar mortal beings, but only from above (ἄνωθεν). Improving our being by intellectual or even spiritual exercises cannot give that unique reality, obtainable only from what is absolute, permanent, everlasting, eternal. It is not a question of becoming more human, or even more religious. The question is how to come into communion with God himself, how to share his glory, his love. Such a movement towards the Creator gives greater hope and security. While for us it was impossible to reach God, God by the Incarnation of his Son made himself accessible (John 3). It is this reality of God's condescension, remaining with us for ever, which we call the Church.

In fact, in becoming a member of the Church, a Christian receives more than he expects. He becomes a partaker of those divine gifts which constitute the very essence of the Church. A Christian becomes one with the Divine Victim, whom he 'consumes' during the Eucharist. This movement towards his archetype, his hidden image of a life previous to the Fall, enables him to overcome the obstacles and reactions of his fallen nature and the hostile forces of the world. What is important is not so much for him to avoid evil and vice, as to become receptive to God's offer to conform his life to that of Christ. Salvation means that a 'new being' is being produced, having all the dimensions of *theōsis*. From that moment, man becomes not only good, in the ordinary sense, but redeemed, liberated and a real child of God, a brother of Christ. No word expresses these dimensions as well as *theōsis*, as defined by Denys the Areopagite:

> '*Theōsis* is assimilation to and union with God to the extent that is permitted. It is the common end of all hierarchy, a continual love of God and of divine things, carried out in a holy way in God and in unity, and previously, the total and irreversible flight from what opposes it, the *gnōsis* of what is as being, the vision and the science of the holy truth, participation in God (*entheos methexis*) in uniform perfection and in the One himself so far as this is permitted, the satisfying intuition that nourishes intellectually whoever tends towards it' (*Hier. Eccles.* 1, 3).

Now such union with the Trinity means union with the divine energies not the divine essence. We do not become the Father or the Son or the Holy Spirit; rather we share so intimately in their life-creating energies that we are joined to them, and that even in this union we still remain ourselves. We have chosen to be joined to the Trinity, Father, Son and Holy Spirit. This is explained clearly by Maximus the Confessor: 'God and those who are worthy of God have one and the same energy' (*Ambigua*; *PG* 91, 1076), i.e. they lovingly conform their will to the will of God.

A *methexis* takes place, by which all blessings stemming from Christ's death and resurrection are transmitted to men. Hence a new life, a real *metamorphōsis* takes place, a new *hypostasis* replaces the 'old man', thanks to the operation of the Holy Spirit. In this framework, ontological as well as soteriological, there must be seen to be set the foundation of the Church on the Holy Trinity. Consequently, sacraments are activities for our human nature connected with the *Logos*, the Word of God made man. There exists, as a result, a mystical identification between the historical Jesus and his body, the Church, which, though operating in time and space, yet elevates its members beyond time into an uncreated reality. This is the fulfilment of the immense *philanthropia* of God to the world.

God as Father in the Church

For a better understanding of our salvation, we must distinguish between two things: the entire economy of redemption as such, i.e. the arrangement of everything required for our salvation, on the one hand, and the actual process of salvation on the other.

Through God's love, infinite and immeasurable, Christ accomplished the former, whilst the latter is carried out through the goodness of the Father, certainly, but by the special mission of the Holy Spirit. For the accomplishment of our salvation, it is necessary that the requirements of salvation, combined in the Person of Christ, be applied to and assimilated by each one of us. We must see how God has called souls at different stages, by different means, and how people have followed this command willingly or unwillingly. In Christ's words, 'none comes to him except as the Father wills it'. We have to recognise here the predominant action of God the Father, who wills every human being to be saved and to come to the knowledge of the truth (2 Tim. 3:7). Begun under the guidance of the Church, through Christ, conversion and renewal are brought to completion under the influence of the Spirit through the grace of the Sacraments, in accordance with the individual activity and various relationships of each person. In this connection, Gregory of Nazianzus says:

> 'If the Spirit be not God, then let it first be divinised, and then make me divine, being equal in honour with him' (*Sermon* 34, 12; *PG* 36, 252).

He goes on to explain the contribution of each person of the Trinity to the divine economy. What we have here is, in other words, a progressive revelation. The revelation of the Spirit in the Church constitutes the summit of the philanthropic revelation of the Holy Trinity to the world. The Ascension of Christ marks the end of his direct action in the world. It is continued through the mission of the Holy Spirit (Greg. Naz., *Sermon* 42, 5; *PG* 36, 436).

The distinction between specific periods in the activity of the Three Persons is generally accepted both by East and West.

Each Person has a special mission and relationship to the world. The Father is the real cause (soul), from which everything proceeds: ὁ ἐξ οὗ τὰ πάντα. The Son is the one through whom all proceeds: ὁ δι' οὗ τὰ πάντα. The Holy Spirit is the principle within which all things have their being: τὸ ἐν ᾧ τὰ πάντα.

This idea of a distribution of tasks is found in John Chrysostom:

'The Father, the Son and the Holy Spirit share the economy for the benefit of human beings' (*Sermon on Pentecost* I, 2; *PG* 50, 456).

So, though manifested in different ways, the mission of the Trinity in the Church is a shared one. John Chrysostom remarks:

'Whenever one *hypostasis* of the Trinity is present, the whole blessed Trinity is there, because it remains unbroken and undivided, united with precise exactitude' (*Homily* 13, 8 on Romans; *PG* 60, 519).

Furthermore, in order to show the inner-Trinitarian relationship, the Fathers introduced the term 'cause', αἴτιον. This supreme Cause or Source, πηγή, refers exclusively to the Father. The Son is begotten from the Substance of the Father, while the Spirit proceeds from this Substance. In other words, the Cause remains single and unique. The Source of divinity is one, namely, the Person of the Father. Gregory of Nyssa distinguishes this 'αἴτιον' or 'cause' from various other definable causes in connection with the inner-Trinitarian relationship:

'Among men, there are many persons, but none owes his being or existence to another person. Each becomes a different person according to the law of product and producer. This is not, however, the case with the Holy Trinity. There is but one Person, namely the Father, from whom the Son is begotten and from whom the Holy Spirit proceeds. This is the main reason why we qualify the one Cause together with what proceeds from this Cause, as the one and unique God' (*Sermon to the Greeks*; *PG* 45, 180).

Later on, Gregory Palamas developed this doctrine, affirming that there is only one Cause in the Trinity, namely, the Father, with two αἰτιατά as the result of this cause.

'If Christ were the cause of the Spirit, he should be called Father' (*Apodeictic Sermons* A, 6).

It can be said that the Father sent his Son into the world that the world through him might be saved (Jn. 3:17), and that the Son sent the Spirit of the Father to perfect his work (Jn. 14:16-17:26). Membership of the Church, therefore, is not so much a doctrine as a way of life, in which separate individuals are so united that their unity can be linked to the inherent oneness of the three Persons. It was for the creation of his One Church among humans that Christ prayed to his Father. The foundation of the unity of human beings in the Church is the Trinitarian Love. This Love remains the permanent model for imitation. Nobody can work out his salvation alone. He needs the Trinity's protection, reflecting the Trinity's inner love, like a mirror-image. Our love and in general our social behaviour towards our fellow-men should reflect the intimate solidarity of the Holy Trinity. As Anthony of Egypt says: 'From our neighbour is life and from our neighbour is death. If we win our neighbour, we win God, but if we cause our neighbour to stumble, then we sin against Christ' (*Apophthegmata* 9). Having shown that the ideal of the Church is the consubstantiality of the Persons of the Trinity, our Lord prayed in the same prayer 'that the love wherewith thou has loved me may be in them and I in them' (Jn. 17:26). Likewise, in his last sermon, Jesus exhorted his disciples to imitate this incomparable mutual Love of the Persons of the Trinity (Jn. 13:34-35).

This inner-Trinitarian relationship of cooperation can be seen in the whole history of Israel. Firstly in the selection of Abraham and the chosen People, then in the lives of Noah, Job, Tobias etc. and, after that, in the embryonic Church of the Gentiles. There is no period of history without an explicit activity of one of the Persons. God is truly 'ecumenical', embracing the whole of humanity. He manifests his love both before and after Moses. He takes care even of those outside Israel (John Chrysostom, *Comment. on Psalm* 113; *PG* 55, 313). Gregory of Nazianzus expresses the view that the existence of the Holy

Spirit had even been discerned by certain Greek philosophers, only they used different names to describe the Spirit, calling it either νοῦς τοῦ παντός, the Mind of the Universe, or θύραθεν νοῦς, the External Mind (*Theol. Oration* 5, 5; *PG* 36, 137).

Because of the activity of the Spirit before the Incarnation, the prophets and righteous are included by the Orthodox Church among the redeemed members of the Church during the liturgical year. As Justin said: 'Whatever has been said before Christ's Incarnation comes from Christians', thus describing the 'spermatic' elements of Truth in ancient Greek philosophy (*Apol.* 2, 13, 3-4).

The Inner Relationship of the Trinity — Σχέσις

We need further investigation as to the mission of the Spirit in this life-giving process.

Is our God the God of Islam or, better still — to go right back to the source — is he essentially the 'one' God of the Jews? Yes, surely, if one refers to Jesus' actual preaching. Did he not answer the good scribe with: 'The first commandment is: Hear, O Israel, the Lord our God, the Lord is one: and thou shalt love the Lord thy God with all thy heart . . . and with all thy strength'? Is not the Gospel in its entirety a witnessing on the part of Jesus to the God of Abraham, Isaac and Jacob, to the one God of the prophets, even if Jesus almost always calls him simply 'Father'?

What is new in Jesus is that this God, this Father, appears singularly alive, singularly near to us, and this precisely in Jesus himself. And soon, in fact, the veil is lifted. After the Resurrection, the disciples finally grasp the stature of Jesus, and the truth of his statement: 'The Father and I are one'. The liturgical hymn included by St. Paul in his letter to the Colossians gives sufficiently dazzling confirmation of this: 'He is the image of the invisible God, the firstborn of all creation; for in him were all things created . . . all things have been created through him and unto him; and he is before all things, and in him all things subsist.'

Nevertheless the relations between the Son (and also between the Holy Spirit), and the Father, as they concern the divine unity, did not initially make themselves evident in intellectual terms. The Trinity, as he expresses himself in the baptismal formula: 'in the name of the Father and of the Son and of the Holy Spirit', is simply experienced within the early Church, which participates actively in him through the Holy Spirit. And the divine unity would appear to be sufficiently safeguarded by the reference to the Father who is πηγὴ τῆς θεότητος, the Source. Nonetheless movements began to come into being which advocated two opposite viewpoints. To affirm fully the Divinity of the Son, some of these movements appeared to reduce him to being no more than a modality of the one God, in brief a symbolic way of evoking God as Creator. Others had more respect for the reality of the Person of the Son, but failed to maintain his full equality with the Father in respect of the divine nature.

It was at this point that Arius appeared on the scene at the start of the 4th Century. The persecutions had just ceased. Christianity which, in its heroic phase, had been in the main an ardent life lived in the Spirit, henceforth left more room for speculation. Thereupon the whole problem of the relationship between the Father, the Source of divine unity, Jesus the Incarnate Word, and the Holy Spirit, manifested itself in all its acuity. Believing he was preserving the unity of God, Arius refused to concede true Divinity to Christ. The Word was only the first among the created, and that creature through which God had created all others.

It was then, and because of this, that the Council of Nicaea took place. Up to this time theological reflection had preferred to consider the mystery of the Faith from the general viewpoint of the Bible, which is the history, above all, of the saving interventions of God. Without doubt, since the coming of Jesus, men were faced with a type of intervention that was both unique and definitive. God, who in former times had spoken by the prophets, had now spoken by his Son, who was his Word, his living Word. The history of salvation did not simply bring into play a distant, thundering God, Yahweh on Sinai, for God showed himself as very close to us in Jesus Christ, his only Son, and in the Holy Spirit. Jesus and the Spirit had the power of divinising. That is why (and there was no possibility of contesting this), they both belonged, along with the Father, to the divine sphere of the Ineffable. There, there can be only One God. And yet the participation of the Father, the Son and the

Spirit in the history of Salvation by creating a new life, the ecclesial life, reveals so manifestly their individual characteristics, that it is impossible not to attribute a distinct reality and distinctive action to each of the three divine Persons, even though the Father remains the Origin, the First.

The heresy of Arius, which contested the Divinity of the Word, was to lead to a greater deepening of awareness of the perfect equality between the Word incarnate and his Father. The Council of Nicaea stated precisely that, in regard to the natures of the Word and the Father, they were identical. And it expressed this fact by using the word *homoousios* — 'consubstantial'. This meant that the Father and the Word do not only have a similar Nature, they possess one and the same identical Nature; they have not only one intelligence, one power, and one outpouring of goodness, but the 'same' intelligence, power and goodness. At the Council of Constantinople some fifty years later (381), the same statement was proclaimed with regard to the Holy Spirit. The Son, when compared with the divine Nature, is identical with the divine Nature. And the same is true of the Holy Spirit. Thus there is in reality one single Divinity, one single God. All that is in God can only be God.

The Council of Nicaea created nothing new. It simply safeguarded the totality of the mystery of salvation by formulating it in wholly safe terms: on the one hand, God in his absolute simplicity and unity; on the other, the Father, the Son and the Holy Spirit, the consubstantial Trinity, revealed by the Father's sending of the Son and of the Holy Spirit so as to ensure our salvation.

The first question is: How can the human mind grasp and assimilate, in the light of the Faith, the distinctiveness of the three divine Persons in the total sameness and identity of the one single divine Nature? And the second question: What link can we establish on the one hand between the Mystery of God, considered in his eternal, sovereign transcendence and, on the other hand, his action during the course of human history, in order to save men? There must exist a bridge between the highest Trinitarian theology, and 'the Economy', that is to say the plan of salvation as realised by God in the Church militant and in history. It is indeed remarkable that it was by the passage among us of the Son of God, become the Son of Man, and by his intimate sharing in our own personal life, that God chose to manifest himself in his inaccessible Mystery, and in his reality as the one and only God in three Persons.

The teaching of the Spirit is not a new revelation, it is an illumination from within. The Spirit penetrates the heart, sensitises the conscience, gives understanding in connection with Church membership. His mission is to guide man 'into all truth' (Jn. 16:13), that is to say, the fullness of the truth grasped in the light of the Faith. Under the guidance of the Spirit man penetrates more deeply into the revealed mystery; he discovers its profundity and its implications in given situations; he finds the strength to respond to the call of the Divine. Filled with the Spirit, the Apostles start to prophesy: they are as if intoxicated (ἔλεγον ὅτι γλεύκους μεμεστωμένοι εἰσί — Acts 2:13). They go forth to announce the Kingdom and the redeeming power of Christ in his Church. For the Spirit is essentially a vital dynamism which guides us and sets us in the heart of truth, that is to say in God himself. It is he who sensitises us to the things from on high and enables us to grasp, through and behind events, the expression of the divine plan of salvation as it develops through the course of history. It is in the Spirit that the new law, the law of love and not of fear, receives its fulfilment.

The Church in God's economy of salvation

There is a widespread belief that to become a member of the Christian family, faith in Christ is enough (Gal. 5:6). There is a grain of truth in that, but Paul clearly maintains that noone can proclaim Jesus Christ except through the Holy Spirit (I Cor. 12:3). This last verse does not refer to the general calling, but to the testimony which follows. In other words, it is not referring exclusively to that operation of the Holy Spirit whereby salvation in Christ is manifested to the sinner who is invited to accept it. It is a fact that a human being cannot remain well-established in the faith outside the Church. Those who confess Jesus as the Lord are those who, in the one Spirit, are baptised into the Body: 'For in one Spirit we were all baptised into one body and we were all made to drink of one Spirit' (I Cor. 12:13). This Baptism is the essential means whereby a person may become a member of the Body of Christ. Nobody is exempted from that; even the Apostles received an exceptional form of Baptism, on the day of Pentecost (Acts I:5).

The importance of the Trinitarian and particularly of the Pneumatological structure of the Church, can be seen from the Fathers' description of it as the 'soul' and 'very heart' of the Church. John Chrysostom says that just as in a body it is the spirit which holds and ordains everything, and makes one single whole out of the different members, so it is here. The Spirit was given so that people of different races and customs might become one (*Homily in Epist. and Ephes.*, 9, 3; *PG* 62, 72). The great Alexandrian theologian Didymus the Blind (313-398) makes a similar statement (*On the Holy Trinity*, 2, 1; *PG* 39, 449).

The task of the Holy Spirit is the gradual formation of the humanly imperfect ecclesiastical body into the Body of Christ, and the incorporation of each of its members into this Body. The Holy Spirit is the life-giving principle of the supernatural life of the Church. He sanctifies, leads to perfection, distributes the various charisms and sustains Christians in their daily struggles. His divine grace descends from the life-pouring Head, Christ, and flows mystically down into the members. The union of the members with the Head and with one another through spiritual rebirth, justification and sanctification, is therefore the work of the Holy Spirit. St. Basil somewhere explains this in detail:

> It is through the Holy Spirit that it is really possible to share the ecclesiastical Tradition — that is, to live as Christians — as throughout history it was believed, because it constituted the prolongation of Christ on earth.

Moreover, Christian life is the continuance of Christ through the work of his grace, by the Holy Spirit, through the generations of believers and those assembled in the spiritual *synaxis*, i.e. those who make up the Church. The Church cannot exist without this close tie between believers and between the successive generations of believers which gives it the authority of Tradition. If this close tie (which is the work of the Holy Spirit) is to exist in Christ, and the Church is to continue to exist thereby, there must be cooperation between all the believers who live in Christ, through the Holy Spirit. So believers do not remain passive in their continuance of Christ, of the work of the Holy Spirit. They become the conscious channel through which life in Christ flows. This current passes among them and unites them on a higher plane with each other. They exercise this function by their confession of faith, their prayers and their common effort to conform their lives to Christ. So the current is transmitted from generation to generation; for, in sending his Son, God's intention was not to produce an isolated event. *Traditio est Christum tradere et in Christo vivere.*

That is why, on the one hand, the Person of Christ and his saving acts constitute the operative content of doctrine. But, on the other hand, the very knowledge of the content of doctrine cannot be separated from its confession, or from the sacraments and the Christian life according to the will and example of Christ. The content of doctrine is, in fact, the core of the Christian testimony and of the confession of faith. Christ appears in these different fruits which are prayer, the sacraments, and life in him, and he is actively present in each of them.

These various elements and activities of the Church constitute an indissoluble whole. Through this complex, the Holy Spirit, who is also the grace of Christ, operates within every man. In each one of them this totality is transmitted. Men are not capable of transmitting the revealed truths by themselves, or of receiving them merely through faith, or of living them. It is impossible for them to do so without the Holy Spirit, that is, without grace. And in turn, the Holy Spirit, or grace, acts through men whose faith is animated by the various components of the Tradition which we have previously enumerated. It is like a chain of spreading warmth. In the Holy Spirit, Christ effects our salvation.

This divine Body, the Church, strictly speaking, does not really begin its life with Christ: it has been united with the eternal Logos from the timeless beginning. It has pre-existed beyond any limitation of time and space, 'hidden' in the mystery of God's economy. It has always existed in the 'wisdom and providence' of God, as Hermas says (*Shepherd* I, 3, 4), as a 'spiritual' Church having an invisible existence. Before the aeons God had conceived of a plan of redemption for mankind's salvation. St. Athanasius rightly says that the Church was first built and afterwards brought to birth by God (*De Incarnatione* 12; *PG* 26, 1004).

In brief, God's eternal plan and will concerning the Church

existed together with his eternal will to create the world and to effect its salvation through his only-begotten Son. The origin, therefore, of the Church is found not on man's side but on God's. Its origin is a divine mystery — supernatural and celestial, not human and earthly. It is an activity of the Trinity, having as Creator God himself (Hebr. 11:10). Thus, as John Chrysostom remarks, 'the real beginning' is in the intention, the will and the impulse of the Father, but its accomplishment is through Christ (*Homily in Ephist. and Ephes.* 1, 4; *PG* 62, 15). 'But because the Father wanted it, does not mean that the Son was inactive ... All activities were common as much for the Father as for the Son.' ('Ο Πατὴρ ἠθέλησε, ὁ Υἱὸς ἐνήργησεν. Κοινὰ Πατρὸς καὶ Υἱοῦ πάντα'.)

All the righteous, from Abel onwards, whether Jews or Gentiles, prepared by stages the coming of the full and perfect Church, the day of Pentecost. Consequently, the angels who remained faithful to God, and later the faithful of all ages, must be considered as members of the Church. Already Ignatius of Antioch referred to its having 'existed before all ages, blessed and predestined for ever to eternal glory' (*Ad Ephes.*, prologue). Clement of Alexandria speaks of the pre-existence of the Church as being the 'first-born' (πρωτότοκος), thus repeating the similar teaching of Hebrews: 'And to the assembly of the first-born who are enrolled in heaven, and to the Judge who is God of all, and to the spirits of just men made perfect' (Hebr. 12:23). Many of the Fathers speak 'of the Apostolic Catholic Church being already from the very beginning, but only completely revealed and made known with Christ's descent among men, in due time', as Epiphanius of Cyprus states (*Contra Haer.* 3, 2; *PG* 42, 640).

It nevertheless remains a complete mystery how God, in remote times and in unseen ways, could manifest his presence and sovereignty over nature and humanity. His aim could only be apprehended by believers after the Passion and Resurrection of Christ. The *Didache* speaks of a 'cosmic mystery' (xi, II). Origen mentions this when he speaks of '*Ecclesiam primitivorum*' (*In Numer. Hom.* 3; *PG* 12, 596). St. Athanasius, combining Christology and ecclesiology in a harmonious synthesis, finds the Church in the eternal plan of God through the intention of the *Logos*, destined to remain with us, as the departure, the foundation of our new creation and rebirth, because the life of

Christians was established and prepared in Christ long before (*Contra Arianos* 2, 75; *PG* 26, 305). Orthodox hymnography has incorporated this belief in the liturgies of St. Basil and St. John Chrysostom, where all the 'resting' saints of the past are commemorated, their intercession is sought, as is that of the angels, for whom special feasts are appointed. Deeply embedded in the conscience of the Orthodox is the belief that the Church extends throughout the *oikoumene*, beyond time and age.

The motivation for this 'cosmic mystery' lies in God's Love. From the very beginning, God intended to create other beings as partakers of the divine blessings. 'Having predestined us unto the adoption of children by Jesus Christ to himself, according to the good pleasure of his will' (Eph. 1:5). Since love implies sharing, God wanted us to share his glory. The whole mystery of his economy is summed up by John Chrysostom: 'He wanted mankind to be seated in the highest, in celestial dwellings, with all the angelic orders' (*In Epist. ad Ephes. Homily* I, 4; *PG* 62, 15). For this task, the Church is invested with all the necessary power, since Christ invested the Apostles with special power and likewise endowed their successors as ministers of reconciliation. It was bearing this in mind that Ignatius of Antioch wrote: 'Wherever Jesus Christ is found, there is also the Catholic Church' (*Ad Smyrn*. 8, 2: *PG* 2, 281: Ὅπου ἂν ᾖ Χριστὸς Ἰησοῦς, ἐκεῖ ἡ Καθολικὴ Ἐκκλησία). Of course, there have been abuses of this affirmation, either by overstating the ministerial element, when the presence of the clergy becomes the sole criterion: *Ubi Ecclesia, ibi Christus*, or by exaggerating the congregational element: *Ubi Christus, ibi Ecclesia* — a distorted reading of Mt. 18:20, as if a simple gathering of believers could attain the status of an ecclesial community.

Though the Three Persons work jointly for the salvation of believers, yet there are instances where one of them takes the initiative, from the human angle, though the Father is always the Source. Soteriology cannot therefore be defined exclusively as Christology or Pneumatology; it remains Trinitarian. It is just such a communion that John Chrysostom has in mind in describing the *methexis* in their blessings:

'God has called us to become partakers of the same gifts, no less; to all he has accorded immortality; to all he has promised life eternal, everlasting glory and brotherhood. On all he has bestowed his heritage. He has become the common Head of all, and to all he has given the same honour. The most essential of all are those gifts commonly available to all, namely Baptism, salvation by faith, having God as Father, the possibility of participating, all, in the same Spirit' (*In Epist. ad Ephes. Hom.* I; *PG* 62, 17).

The particular cosmic mission of the Spirit in the Church

As the Church is a product of the Spirit's activity, the article in the Nicene Creed, on the 'One, Holy, Catholic and Apostolic Church' follows immediately on the confession of the Holy Spirit.

It is thus made evident that the work of spiritual rebirth, sanctification and illumination is performed in unison by the Father, the Son and the Holy Spirit. There is no claim that the Spirit alone has the power to sanctify. Basil of Caesarea declares that all three Persons are equally sanctifying, and that none is less active or of secondary importance (*Letter* 109, *PG* 32, 693). The Spirit never acts alone but always jointly with the other two Persons of the Blessed Trinity, so that the Church as a whole and each of its members individually always remain within the unbroken and undivided sovereignty of the whole Trinity. As St. John Chrysostom teaches, 'the actions of the Trinity are inseparable. Where there is communion of the Spirit, there will also be communion of the Son. And where the action of the Son, Jesus Christ, is operative, there also is the action of the Father and the Holy Spirit' (*Comm. on 2 Cor., Hom.* 30, 2; *PG* 61, 608).

While the Spirit is given so that his blessings may permeate all liturgical acts, he is also indwelt personally by Christians who struggle constantly to this end. It is worth recalling that in the 4th century, when the Massalians launched an anti-ecclesiastical and anti-liturgical spirituality, there was a real danger of falling into a humanistic set of morals. This error originated with the early 4th century Massalians or Euchites, who denied any assistance from sacramental life and relied on the merits of self-sufficient piety or individual prayer (*myriaskēsis*). Another unhealthy facet of their spirituality was equally dangerous: a moral *imitatio* of Christ and the saints, a kind of mimetism or *habitus*. What the Fathers affirmed was not a simple improvement of human nature but a second birth, a radical regeneration, a *theōsis* and 'newness of life', a 'christification' of all our being. Thus in Orthodox hymnography, the prayer of the Festival of Pentecost (3rd prayer) is addressed to the Fount of all gifts:

> 'O God, who on this redeeming day of the Pentecostal Feast didst reveal unto us the mystery of the Holy Trinity as one in Essence, co-eternal, undivided and unmingled, and didst pour out the holy and life-giving Spirit in the form of tongues of fire upon thine holy apostles, and didst appoint the same to be heralds of the glad tidings of our holy faith, and didst make them confessors, . . . hear us . . .'.

Yet the Spirit could not perform this service unless he derived the power to do so from the Father, and to manifest it through the Son, or if the Son did not manifest it through the Spirit. Each operation fulfils its end because the perfect communion in God, which exists not only in the common Essence but also in each divine operation, is manifested and accomplished in the Third Person of the Trinity. It is clear to us, therefore, that the Spirit plays an extremely important role in the relationship which God the Father has established with his creation in accomplishing its salvation.

In practical daily life, the love of God and a sense of responsibility for this life are the work of the Spirit. Where this life is pure, this takes the form of adoration, or when we realise our sinfulness and disobedience to the supreme Will, the form of trembling fear and tremendous awe. Only the Spirit can awaken in us an appropriate response to the loving invitation of the Father, which is conveyed to us by the same Spirit. Only the Spirit can give to this response its fervour and joy. Only the Spirit can make us share the Son's sensitivity and sense of responsibility to the Father.

The indwelling and operation of the Spirit in the human soul is the essential mission and role of the Spirit. By its nature, the soul is prepared for this visit and unique communion. As an expression of the human *hypostasis*, the soul is the image of the *Logos* and, by the Spirit's natural attraction towards the Person of the Father, it has this tendency in itself from the very beginning. Our soul expects to be visited by the Spirit, to be loved, to be completed. Sin, by weakening this desire to relate to the supreme Person and to other (human) persons, has placed the soul in an embarrassing situation, in a state contrary to its nature. The indwelling of the Spirit thus re-establishes and strengthens the soul in its capacity to relate to God and fellow human beings. In other words, the Spirit restores the soul (when disfigured) to its nature and original beauty (*pros to ek physeos kallos*), according to the profound remark of Basil of Caesarea (*De Spiritu Sancto*; *PG* 32, 109). 'The *apokatastasis* (reinstatement) in Paradise is due to the Holy Spirit; it implies ascension into the Kingdom of Heaven, return to sonship, the privilege of invoking God as one's Father, the partaking of the grace of Christ, becoming children of light, participating in the divine glory, and in general being filled with blessings of all kinds during this life and in the life to come' (*De Spiritu Sancto* 15, 36; *PG* 32, 129). From the day of Pentecost on, a new era begins for Christ's followers. Time acquires a different meaning. Though inaccessible, God becomes henceforth both transcendent and immanent. The coming of the Paraclete constitutes for the Church the guarantee and the beginning of a new relationship, with the eternal blessings becoming real and accessible to every human being. Eschatology is therefore not an isolated, distant attribute, but an existential and empirical reality. The saving operation of God, through Christ in the Holy Spirit, makes *theōsis* a tangible experience, manifested now but to be completed at the *Parousia*, the Second Coming.

The Holy Spirit acts in a twofold way. He sanctifies and leads believers to the wholeness of truth (Jn. 16:13). Through sanctification, he makes us partakers of God's holiness, enabling us to fight against sin. And through the truth of the Christian faith, he protects us from error. It would be impossible for us to achieve these aims of the Holy Spirit by our own strength, because truth and holiness are two qualities connected exclusively with God. But God in his goodness 'wills that all should be saved and come to the knowledge of the truth' (I Tim. 2:4). He reveals the truth to all who believe in him, in order that they may know his Will, and subsequently fight against the error existing in the present world. Error is personified by Satan (the

Deceiver) who from the beginning is the father of lies (Jn. 8:44), i.e. who schemes to spread lies all around. Guided by the Holy Spirit, Patristic theology aimed precisely at formulating the True Faith, in order to resist its distortion, i.e. heresy. The mission and existence of the Church are closely related to the continuous presence of the Holy Spirit. This belief is of vital importance, for the Fathers admitted it could happen that a church might turn away from the Spirit and depart from the Truth. In that case, we have a dead body, cut off from communion with God. St. John Chrysostom comments:

> 'If the Spirit had not been present, the Church would not have come into being. If a local church is constituted, it is evident that the Spirit is there' (*Homily on Pentecost*; *PG* 50, 459).

The Spirit continues the redeeming work of Christ, by transmitting to each member of the Church the fruits of redemption. Without the presence of the Holy Spirit, the assumption by Christ of human nature would have been ineffective, or effective only as an historical event of the past. The problem is how to perpetuate 'unto all ages' this redemption accomplished once and for all, *ephapax*, by Christ. Here we see the importance of the Spirit for the very birth and accomplishment of the Church's mission.

As Origen pointed out, without the sanctifying means of the Church, nobody can be saved, and we are led to death (*Comment. in Jesu Nav.* 5, 3, 5; *PG* 12, 481). This explains why, for Irenaeus, the inauguration of the Church's mission is identified with the particular operation of the Holy Spirit (*Contra Haer.* 3, 24; *PG* 7, 966). The Church and the Holy Spirit are ontologically connected. What precedes is the reconciliation of God with humanity through Christ. Afterwards, the Holy Spirit is given as a token of reconciliation, as St. John Chrysostom correctly observed (*Sermon on Pentecost* I, 3; *PG* 50, 457).

It is generally accepted by the Fathers that in the whole creation, visible and invisible, rational and irrational, the Spirit is the sustaining element of the structure of being, harmonising the conflicting elements in nature. This operation provides a permanent friendship with creation, which the Spirit does not permit to disintegrate but supports with all his cohesive power.

No created thing contains the cause of life within itself, nor can any created thing produce this cause. If deprived of the Spirit even for an instant, creation dies. The maintenance (*syntērēsis*) of the world is the work of the Spirit (*On the Holy Trinity*, 2, 7, I; *PG* 39, 452). This explains why the Spirit is described as co-Creator (*syndēmiourgos*), and fellow- (lit. equal) worker (*isourgos*).

The manifold mission of the Spirit is reflected in Orthodox worship which regards all things as able to receive the sanctifying grace of the Spirit, and in this way to contribute to the 'liturgical cosmic function'. All sacraments have a material shape. The power of the Spirit uses the earthly visible elements.

The Trinity in Worship

That the whole Trinity is engaged in the common task of guiding all men towards salvation, is affirmed above all in Orthodox worship. Every religious service invokes, with rare exceptions, the Trinity. The most ancient and frequent Trinitarian formula: 'In the name of the Father, and of the Son and of the Holy Spirit', illustrates the involvement of the whole Trinity in hearkening to our prayers and responding to our petitions. Again, in regular morning prayer, we address our supplications to the Trinity:

> 'Most Holy Trinity, have mercy on us. O Lord, wash away our sins. O Master, pardon our transgressions. O Holy One, visit and heal our infirmities, for thy Name's sake.'

And during Vespers we sing:

> 'Glad light of the holy glory of the immortal, heavenly, holy and blessed Father, Jesus Christ, now that we have come to the setting of the sun and have seen the evening light, we praise God: Father, Son and Holy Spirit. It is meet at all times to praise Thee with happy voices, O Son of God and Giver of Life. Therefore the world glorifies thee.'

Again, at the end of each Divine Liturgy, the Trinity is explicitly hymned in the joyful exclamations of the faithful:

'We have seen the true Light; we have received the
heavenly Spirit; we have found the true Faith,
worshipping the undivided Trinity; for this has saved us.'

One can conclude that the whole blessed Trinity is the Head
of the Church and its supreme cause and source of grace and
substance, as John Chrysostom teaches on this score: 'Πατρὸς
καὶ Υἱοῦ καὶ Πνεύματος ἁγίου μία ἡ δωρεὰ καὶ ἐξουσία' —
Comment. in Johan. hom. 86, 3; *PG* 59, 471.

In recalling the wonders of Christ's Resurrection, with the
early visit of the Myrrh-bearing Women, a Trinitarian hymn is
added:

'We adore the Father and His Son and the Holy Spirit,
the Holy Trinity in one Essence, crying with the
Seraphim: Holy, Holy, Holy art thou, O Lord.' (Mattins,
Evlogitaria of the Resurrection, tone 5).

In the *Gloria in Excelsis*, or Great Doxology, there is developed a
paean of praise to the Trinity:

'O Lord God, heavenly King, Father Almighty; O Lord,
only-begotten Son, Jesus Christ, and Holy Spirit. O Lord
God, Lamb of God, Son of the Father, who takest away
the sin of the world, have mercy on us. . . . Thou who
sittest at the right hand of the Father, have mercy on us.
For thou only art holy, thou only art the Lord, Jesus
Christ, in the glory of God the Father . . .'

Solemnly, the Eucharist begins by blessing the reign of the
Holy Trinity. All the *ekphoneses* concluding the liturgical prayers
jointly render honour, adoration and glory to the Trinity, for to
those Persons belong the dominion, the kingdom and the power.
The *Epiclēsis* constitutes another element emphasising the
Spirit's essential action in sanctifying the Divine Gifts. And
throughout the hymnography of Lent and Easter (*Triodion,
Pentecostarion*), is attached a special group of hymns extolling the
Trinitarian economy, known as '*Triadika*'.

In general, the Trinitarian formula, under various guises,
appears in the liturgy, eucharistic or other. All hymnography is
plunged in a deep faith in the Trinity's unique ability to sustain
the community of believers in their struggle with evil, and in

their effort to become children of the Kingdom. One of the most significant *troparia* of the feast of the Epiphany states:

> 'When in Jordan thou wast baptised, O Lord, the worship of the Trinity was made manifest. For the voice of the Father bare witness unto thee, calling thee his beloved Son, and the Spirit, in the form of a Dove, confirmed the steadfastness of that word' (*Apolytikion*, tone 1).

In similar terms the hymnographer describes, extolling the nativity in flesh of Christ, the Trinitarian action for the redemption of all creation:

> 'Hearken, O heaven, and give ear, O earth: for behold, the Son and Word of God the Father comes forth to be born of a Maiden who has not known man, by the good pleasure of the Father who begat him impassibly, and by the cooperation of the Holy Spirit. Make ready, O Bethlehem: throw open thy gate, O Eden. For he who is, comes to be that which he was not, And he who formed all creation takes form, granting the world great mercy.'
> (Vespers, *Aposticha*, tone 1).

This is not a new discovery, but a more empirical acquaintance with the Faith. What was mere doctrine has now been translated into actual experience; an experience of redemption. We distinguish more clearly the interrelation between doctrine and daily experience, that freshens and revitalises our faith in God. Theology is necessary, but it is no substitute for an intimate relationship with the Holy Trinity. Worshipping the indivisible Trinity is the only worship acceptable to God. The Orthodox do not live only with hope. Salvation is a present reality, although it is perfected and consummated when 'this mortal puts on immortality and this corruptible puts on incorruptibility'.

To sum up: The Church receives her life and saving ministry from the Trinity. It is ever-present in her life and activities. It alone enables her to fulfil her mission and to overcome all adversity. Without the continuous sustaining action of the Trinity, the Church would have been overwhelmed long ago by heresies, aggressions and persecutions.

Finally, as a society of believers, the Church remains in real continuity with her very origins. Liturgical life is not something new. It is the continuous transmission of that which existed in the Church from the very beginning.

Sharing the Cross and the Glory

It is the apostolic teaching embodied in the tradition of the Church, and especially the Eucharist, which together constitute the basis of our faith. In his 'Confession of Faith', annexed to his letter *To Dionysius*, Gregory Palamas states characteristically the following: 'We maintain all the ecclesiastical traditions, both the written and the unwritten, and above all the most mystical and sacred communion (τὴν μυστικωτάτην κοινωνίαν καὶ σύναξιν), the '*synaxis*' in which the other ceremonies are perfected ... Those who do not confess or believe in the manner that the Holy Spirit predicted through the prophets, as the Lord proclaimed when he appeared to us in flesh, as the apostles preached, having been sent by him, as our forefathers and their successors taught us, — they are fallen into heresy ... We disapprove of them and anathematise them' (*Works*, vol. 2, p. 497). Already the acknowledgment of the Eucharist as the basis of Church life helps maintain the unity of theology, and gives it a dynamic aspect. From the very beginning, the Church associated her faith and hope in the Kingdom of God with the Eucharist. For, being the sacrament of the communion of God with men, it constitutes the boundless capital on which the Church continually draws. Palamas, referring to the same sacrament, says: 'At the same time, we are nourished and instructed through it at the same time' (ὁμοῦ τε γὰρ τρεφόμεθα παρ' αὐτοῦ καί διδασκόμεθα — *Homily* 56, 10, ed. S. Economou, p. 211).

The Eucharist, as a sacrament, contains a very deep spiritual meaning. That is why one must not stop at its ritual appearance, but penetrate into its depths. The same applies to anything which reveals the presence of God in history. In order to understand the presence of God, we need the Spirit of God. And to receive the Spirit of God, we must subdue this earthly spirit and submit to the Will of God. When man stops living for himself and lives for God, when the time of his life is not the secular time, the χρόνος which measures his biological and psychological changes, but is the 'transformed' time, which extends with his spiritual maturity and incorporation into the transcending eternal presence of God, he sees everything in a new light, with new dimensions and perspectives. That is why the presence of 'spiritual' men in the world is such an important reminder. Attached to the Tradition, with the Eucharist as its heart (cf. I Cor. 11:23-25), they witness to their faith under all circumstances with the power of conviction.

This eschatological and triumphal dimension of the Eucharist may lead those who attach excessive weight to the coming glory promised through Holy Communion, to go too far. Certainly a Christian shares in the victory of Christ while he partakes of the heavenly food. But since on earth he cannot escape its presupposition, i.e. suffering and the Cross, he has to experience pain and Calvary as much as God asks him to, yet drawing on the Eucharist for strength. (Hence the greeting Βοήθειά σου! extended in Greek parishes to communicants after the Liturgy.) Thus he shows the inseparability of these two elements of Christ's earthly ministry: sacrifice and glory, Golgotha and Resurrection. The Eucharist is no substitute for the costly life of co-suffering and co-crucifixion with the unique One, our Saviour.

Despite this, there are church members who misinterpret the relationship of passion to glory in the Eucharist, tending thereby to eliminate pain from life and so departing from true Christian spirituality. They do all they can to rule out poverty, privations and trials from their lives, as an experience of Christ. They live a cocooned existence, minus the Cross, as if the liturgical life automatically removed pain and bolstered illusions. Nobody can avoid the path trodden by Christ, because pain remains a real test of faithfulness to our calling. The Eucharist, on the other hand, enables us not to drown in the abyss of pain, but to raise our eyes to what is coming thereafter, the *theōsis*, the inheritance of the glories promised.

The most obvious implication of the Eucharistic eschatology combines a memorial (*Anamnēsis*) and a sacrifice. *Anamnēsis* implies the re-enactment of past events and the anticipation of future realities in the present. Such an approach has helped theology to overcome the difficulties created by the classical question of whether the *Anamnēsis* is a repetition or not of a past event, and to regard the Eucharist as a *leitourgia*, the combined action of God and man, as a movement, a passage of the Church from this to the future aeon. To be remembered by God in his Kingdom is, in this case, the crucial part of the Eucharist. The Anaphora, the Offertory, is centred on the *Anamnēsis* of Christ, but this *Anamnēsis* is not just an *Anamnēsis* of the past. It is rather an *Anamnēsis* of the future and of the past only in a future perspective. In the Divine Liturgy of St John Chrysostom, we come across a paradoxical statement: 'we remember ... the second coming, the *parousia*' — a statement that overthrows all the classical scholastic problems concerning the meaning of the Eucharist as a memorial. At the foot of the Cross, we turn our hearts towards the promised joy and glory experienced already by reflecting that we shall see 'face to face' the God whom we now bear sacramentally in our hearts.

What the Church does in the Eucharist is to set the eschatological scene in which the saving acts of God, above all the sacrifice of Christ, are 'remembered by God', which means they acquire the finality and ultimacy which God gives to whatever will finally survive in eternal life. It is in and through this remembrance that the Church commemorates the saints, praying that the entire community, together with the entire cosmos, will be remembered with Christ eternally by God. This means that they will acquire the ultimacy of existence, immortality and eternal life. In this sense the phrase of Ignatius of Antioch: 'partaking of the medicine of immortality' (*Ephes.* 20:2), and that of Serapion: 'the medicine of life' (*Euchologion* 13, 15), acquire their real connotation. The Eucharist does not basically transmit grace as a sort of power flowing from the Cross through a visible channel. Rather it takes us into the eschatological remembrance of Christ by God in which we are assured that we will not die, but will live eternally with his Son.

It is in the context of this eschatological approach that the Eucharist comes into possession of a cosmic dimension. The bread and wine offered during Holy Communion, these very fruits of the earth and the labour of man, are transformed into Christ's Body, precisely because of the eschatological nature of the Eucharist. Just as the *synaxis* is changed into Christ's Body in and through the fact that it will be remembered by God through Christ, in his Kingdom, and will thus survive eternally, so the entire natural cosmos which man brings with him to the

Eucharist will be changed from being mortal to being immortal; it will partake of *theōsis* and so live eternally.

In this way the Eucharist possesses a dimension which outstrips the problem of redemption. It becomes a proclamation of ontology, of the ultimacy of being, of the actual creation's survival. This change of the eucharistic elements is absolutely true and real, not because of any changes that may have taken place in the elements themselves through processes analogous to those of the existing laws of nature (transubstantiation, etc.), but because it is absolutely true and real that whatever is assumed by Christ will be remembered by God and thus will live eternally as Christ's Body. Maximus the Confessor, in this respect, was right concerning the *eschata* and identifying them with the 'Truth'.

None better than Gregory Nazianzen has sung the implications of the Trinity in the Christian *Pascha*:

'The Lord's Passover, the Passover, and again I say the Passover to the honour of the Trinity. This is to us a Feast of feasts and a Solemnity of solemnities as far exalted above all others (not only those which are merely human and creep on the ground, but even those which are of Christ himself, and are celebrated in his honour) as the sun is above the stars. Beautiful indeed yesterday was our splendid array, and our illumination, in which both in public and in private we associated ourselves, every kind of men, and almost every rank, illuminating the night with our crowded fires, formed after the fashion of that great light, both that with which the heaven above us lights its beacons, and that which is above the heavens, amid the angels (the first luminous nature, next to the first Nature of all, because springing directly from it), and that which is in the Trinity, from which all light derives its being, parted from the undivided light and honoured. But today's is more beautiful and more illustrious; inasmuch as yesterday's light was a forerunner of the rising of the Great Light, and, as it were, a kind of rejoicing in preparation for the Festival; but today we are celebrating the Resurrection itself, no longer as an object of expectation, but as having already come to pass, and gathering the whole world unto itself. Let then different persons bring forth different fruits and offer different offerings at this season, smaller or greater ... such spiritual offerings as are dear to God ... as each may have power.' (*Oratio* XLV/*The Second Oration on Easter*, 2; *PG* 36, 624-625).

The consequent authority of the Church

God is never alone. He is bound to his people, through his promises, because above all he is Love. Consequently, the Church can never be alone. Since Christ's Incarnation, she remains inseparably united with him, the Body with the Head, the Bride with the Bridegroom. This mystical union is manifested in Christ's constant care for his Church, which will never perish, despite so many evils in the world, despite the assaults of demonic forces. The Church is divine and human. As composed of human elements she will inevitably show shortcomings and deficiencies on the human side; on the contrary, the divine side of the Church is protected from error. This fact gives the Church the authority to interpret the Faith, i.e. to make visible the plan of God for the salvation of humanity at all times, without human distortion.

Once we accept the permanent indwelling and active presence of the Holy Trinity in the saving mission of the Church, we can easily conclude that she possesses the authority to discern sound doctrine from false. Referring to such unquestionable credibility, Irenaeus stated that all the *kērygma* of truth that the Church had received from the Apostles and their disciples, she preserves with vigilant care (ἐπιμελῶς φυλάσσει τὸ κήρυγμα τοῦτο τῆς ἀληθείας) as if she had one mouth only. In spite of the dissimilarities in the languages of the world, the power of the *Paradosis* remains one and the same (ἡ δύναμις τῆς παραδόσεως μία καὶ ἡ αὐτή — *Contra Haer.*, *lib.* I, 10, 2; *PG* 7, 552).

How, despite so many attacks by pagans, by heretics one after the other, by unworthy bishops who even surrendered to heretical bodies, did the Church remain true, one and apostolic? The answer is found in the fact that, in spite of radical changes and upheavals, she was protected and guided in all the vicissitudes of history by the blessed Trinity. Thus, remaining faithful to her commission, the Church did not abuse this privilege, by adding anything new or by removing elements of the apostolic *didaskalia*. In this fact lies her authority. She relies upon Christ's promise to remain with his disciples to the end of time: 'Lo, I am with you always, even unto the end of the world' (Mat. 28:30). Anticipating sad stormy days for his People, Christ foretold his sending to them of 'the Paraclete, the Spirit of truth, whom the Father will send in my name, he shall teach you all things, and bring all things to your remembrance, whatsoever I have said unto you' (Jn. 14:26).

How, then, after all these solemn promises, can such a body err and act against the original plan for the salvation of the world, established by the Holy Trinity together? For this precise reason, St. Paul qualifies the Church as 'the Church of the living God, the pillar and ground of the truth' (I Tim. 3:15). It is in this context that Theophilus of Antioch compared the scattered local churches to 'inhabited islands surrounded by water, offering hospitable bays and safe harbours as secure refuge to those who are in danger. In these, one can find the teachings of truth, like a haven, to which proceed those who want to be saved, while out of them retreat only wrong teachings, that is, the heresies, which completely destroy those who teach them' (*Ad Autolycum* II, 14; *PG* 5, 32).

More particularly, this guardianship of the Truth is entrusted, not to a particular class, that is, the clergy or *magisterium* alone, but both to the clergy and to the whole *Laos* or *plēroma*. All the baptised are co-responsible for safeguarding the Truth. They are committed to defend the Faith and to participate in a concrete missionary effort for its expansion. By its very nature, the Church is not static: it is called to growth, increase, multiplication. Orthodox ecclesiology has never overlooked the general priesthood of believers, but heeds the text: '... you have an unction from the Holy One, and you know all things' (I Jn. 2:20). There are many instances in Church history, where simple lay-people defended Orthodoxy from the perils of heresy. They were 'the learned of God' (διδακτοὶ θειοῦ), prophets and charismatic bearers of the Spirit. When the Orthodox Church refused to participate in the 1st Vatican Council, the Patriarchs wrote in answer to the Roman invitation an encyclical letter, dated 6 May 1868, declaring that 'the guardian of Orthodoxy is the main body of the Church, that is the people itself'. Neither clergy nor laity alone can be considered as representing the voice of the Church, but only the two together.

The concrete expression of this harmony is the Synod and its reception. An ecumenical gathering has all the necessary prerogatives to reformulate the Faith in up-to-date terms, dealing with disciplinary matters in order to meet urgent needs. As a living organism, the Church must, from time to time, use a new language, with more appropriate expressions, without departing from the *Paradosis*, and adapting previous conciliar decisions to new given situations. No bishop, evidently, can claim absolute, supreme authority over the others, still less over the body of the universal Christian Community. It is the gathering of all in conciliar form, continuing the process of the previous synods, which alone can decide on matters concerning discipline and canonical order, emerging from new conditions and developments. This body does not introduce any new element into that contained in the divine revelation, but simply relates the *vetera* to the *nova*. Its rulings must be in full harmony with preceding ones. There must be a full consensus in this respect. Synods convoked under pressure from the State, and/or manipulated by schismatics, have never gained the necessary credibility and authority. In relating the circumstances of the 1st Ecumenical Council of Nicaea, Athanasius insists that the assembled Fathers 'did not create that wording by themselves, but restated what they had previously received. True understanding was thus passed on from Fathers to Fathers' (ἐκ Πατέρων εἰς Πατέρας διαβέβηκεν ἡ διάνοια). 'The faith which the Synod confessed in written form is indeed that of the catholic Church' (*Letter to the Ascetics*, 36; *PG* 25, 736).

In this respect, one must point out the function of the laity during a synod. Let us recall the proceedings of the first council of Jerusalem, where the Apostles were wrestling with the questions concerning circumcision and the validity of baptism in Christ: 'Then it pleased the apostles and elders, with the whole church . . .' (Acts 15:22). Since then, in many cases, the laity has been represented in conciliary debates, thus contributing to a fuller understanding of the task before them. Nevertheless, it must be admitted that the decisive factor for validity is not the voting of the people through their representatives, the bishops. What actually occurs is that the synodical assembly, fully conscious of interpreting the catholic conscience, makes its decisions as guided by the Holy Spirit; the laity is afterwards called upon to endorse the findings as being in conformity with the undivided faith, voice and conscience of the Church.

This was the process adopted in the case of the 1st, 4th and 7th Ecumenical Councils, approved not immediately but later, often with many hesitations, after controversies and much opposition. This reserved attitude of the people clearly shows that during the debates the Councils did not ask for a kind of referendum. At the time, the laity was not called upon either to approve or to disapprove the proposed decisions; but their following consent constituted weighty evidence of agreement and a witness to their legitimacy (the *sensus fidelium*). The value of lay recognition lies, therefore, in the fact that a synod has operated within a framework of continuity of the uninterrupted Apostolic Faith — the Faith given by the indivisible Trinity.

Practical effects of the Trinitarian mystery

The neglect of the Trinitarian dogma in the West, controlled by the heavy scholastic teaching, resulted in a monolithic, stagnant theology, without the dynamic *energeia* of the Triune God in life and in history. Gregory Palamas already pointed out how damaging was such an immobilism. Repeatedly he recalled that our God is ever-present, acting through the energies communicating his Love to us, in what Patristic theology calls *divine economy*. It is the continuous realisation of the two parallel *missions* (ἐκπορεύσεις) of the incarnate Son and of the Spirit that gives us access to an understanding of the divine Life in its two processions. In fact, our faith holds that the mystery of God's Love is revealed to us by the two events: namely the Incarnation and the sending of the Spirit. (See the promising reflections of B. Fraigneau-Julien: 'Le Dieu vivant donne aux hommes sa Parole dans l'Espirit', *N. Revue Théologique* 4 (1982) 481-494).

Thus the Church is seen as the Body of Christ: both as an *Ecclesia de Trinitate* and as an *Ecclesia de hominibus*, in the continuous presence of the Spirit. The renewal of the Church and the sanctification of its members are worked out by the

Eucharist and the impulse of the Spirit. Consequently, Tradition is no longer seen as a petrified *summum* of doctrines, a mere faithful memory. Above all, it is a living actualisation of the past, a true *anamnēsis*, a *synthesis* between what is transmitted and present experience, brought about by the *Epiclēsis* of the Spirit. Certainly it is a deposit, but, as Irenaeus says: 'a deposit that is always new, rejuvenating the vessel of the expressions in which it is found'. The Spirit unceasingly tells man what to do. Thus the wide area of the world and the whole cosmos is also that of the action of the Spirit. All the NT texts referring to Christ's relationship with the Father manifest the immense expression of his *kenōsis* for the benefit of humanity, but always with equality (ἰσοτιμία). It is rather a self-emptying, a descent (καταβέβηκεν ἐξ ὑπεροχῆς εἰς ἐλάττωσιν), according to John Chrysostom (*Hom. 38 on St. John*; cf. Cyril of Alexandria, *Comment. in Johan.*; *PG* 73, 349). Cyril of Jerusalem explains to the Catechumens how the Spirit is in full action, ever-living and ever-present (ζῶν καὶ συμπαρόν) with the Father and the Son (*Catechesis* 17, 5; *PG* 33, 973). Gregory of Nyssa underlines the Spirit's continuous concern for humanity: self-moving, active (αὐτοκίνητος καὶ ἐνεργός), always seeking goodness and bringing to goodwill the power of doing (*Oratio Catechet.* 2; *PG* 45, 17).

Such is the economy in which the permanent articulation of the mission of the Son and the mission of the Spirit constitute the earthly expression of the processions of the Holy Trinity (γέννησις, ἐκπόρευσις, προβολή). Against the static approach and atrophy caused by maintaining that Christians are formed by sanctifying impersonal *graces*, emphasis is now put on a personal *koinōnia* with the Trinity. No longer *graces instituted* or even inspired by the institution, but real *methexis* in God making salvation available to us, an empirical reality. The Bible henceforth becomes a living voice, word, logos, as Origen states:

> 'This Scripture we are trying at this moment to interpret
> is in fact "word". This is what happened in the Churches
> of Christ: that which was before letters, and was
> understood according to the letter, thanks to the
> revelation of the Lord became Word'. (*In Jesu Nave Hom.*
> 20, 5; *SC* 71, 423).

God speaks today. He comes out of himself in order to be truly man, man like men, Emmanuel. Although the Trinity reaches us, we are still unable to enter into his *ousia*. Here apophatism is needed.

Any inquiry, therefore, neglecting certain limits, might lead to a God of deism, part of the heritage of the degenerate metaphysics of the philosophy of the Enlightenment, supplied on the one hand by the Aristotelian philosophy of *pure Act*, and on the other by the supreme Idea of Plato. The anachronistic theology of the *De Deo Uno* and the metaphysical Christology, without reference to the history of God's salvation, *salus mundi*, had disastrous effects: namely, that of an Almighty Arbiter of human destiny, Guarantor of the established order, a God immovable and impassible in his eternity, in no way involved in the sufferings of his creatures or in human history as a whole. This deism dominated the fearful devotion of the last two centuries.

God is Communion. The Father has given everything to the Son and the gift is the very life of God. And the Spirit leads to the truth, the revelation of the depths of God. This explains why the early Church refused the *subordinationist* principle, derived from a misunderstanding of the divine *monarchy*, the unity of the principle which does not arise in God from inferiority. The Son's obedience — and thus all Christian obedience — is receiving freely and not *submitting himself*. 'Receiving' escapes the logic of domination and submission and becomes life in common. A Church which introduces subordinationism into itself shows that it has not understood the depths of the mystery of *perichōrēsis*. This Trinitarian interaction remains nevertheless a mystery. Thus John of Damascus was right in admitting the incomprehensibility of the Spirit's existence, as being beyond knowledge for us, as is also the begetting of the Son from the Father as Godhead (*De Fide Orthodoxa* I, 8; *PG* 94, 816).

CONCLUDING AFFIRMATION

*Agreed Understanding of the Theological Development and Eventual
Direction of the Orthodox/Reformed Conversations Leading to Dialogue*

In March 1977 an approach was made by the World Alliance
of Reformed Churches to the Ecumenical Patriarch, and the
other Patriarchs and Archbishops in Greece, Cyprus, Egypt and
Jerusalem, with a view to opening up a dialogue between the
Orthodox and the Reformed Churches bearing on the very
centre of the Catholic Faith beginning with the doctrine of the
Holy Trinity. What was proposed was not the usual kind of
ecumenical dialogue concerned with comparative beliefs and
ecclesiologies, but something far more basic, which could affect
all Christendom, through a deep-going clarification of the mind
of the Church regarding the ultimate ground and structure of
the faith on the doctrine of the Holy Trinity.

After the warm welcome and blessing of all the Leaders of the
Orthodox Church, an invitation was extended by His All-
Holiness Dimitrios I to the Reformed Church to send a
delegation to Istanbul in July 1979. Papers were then presented
by the Reformed Delegation spelling out the kind of dialogue
envisaged and the advantage of making the doctrine of the Holy
Trinity the starting point and the controlling theme for all
further consultation in a way that could cut behind traditional
divergences, not only between the Orthodox and the Reformed,
but between the Eastern and Western Church, the Evangelical
and Catholic Churches, and even between the historical
contrapositions of Antiochian and Alexandrian, Chalcedonian
and non-Chalcedonian approaches to Christology and Soteriology — and not least the problems that gave rise to the disunion
of East and West on the *filioque* clause. At the same time it was
suggested that a basic consensus regarding the doctrine of the
Holy Trinity would go far to providing a common basis for
agreed understanding and practice regarding authority in the
Church, and the formulation and development of Christian
Doctrines.

At the first meeting in Istanbul the proposal to make the doctrine of the Holy Trinity the primary theme was received with much satisfaction and was endorsed by the Orthodox Representatives as the correct starting point for continued consultations, although it was recognised that further clarification was needed before firm proposals for formal dialogue could be made.

Further meetings of a preparatory nature took place in Geneva in February 1981 and in March 1983, at which deep soundings were taken by both sides to see if there were sufficient common ground regarding the canon of truth, the nature and the place of authority in the Church, as well as the Trinitarian foundation and character of the Faith. It was felt that if a consensus between the Orthodox and Reformed emerged that was deep enough, it would allow proposals for formal dialogue to go ahead with the doctrine of the Holy Trinity as the basic and predominant theme, which could then be put to the Orthodox and Reformed authorities concerned. In this event, discussion could move out fruitfully from the doctrine of the Holy Trinity to other areas of Christian doctrine where clarifications and ecumenical rapprochement are needed — i.e. through doctrines of Christ and the Holy Spirit to the doctrines of the Church, the Eucharist and the Ministry; but not least to the deep inter-relation between the Incarnation and the Creation, where widespread clarification is urgent for the life and thought, the mission and activity of the Church in the modern scientific world.

At the final consultations in Geneva primary stress was again laid on the doctrine of the Holy Trinity and the Trinitarian perspective for the whole life and faith of the Church, but it was agreed that the bearing of the Trinitarian perspective especially on the identity, structure and authority of the Church had to be kept in mind throughout and allowed to have its full weight.